The
Made
from
Scratch
Life

Melissa K. Norris

Cover by Harvest House Publishers Inc.

Cover photos © Perkus, enviromantic, Julia_Sudnitskaya / iStock

Published in association with the literary agency of WordServe Literary Group, Ltd., www.wordserveliterary.com.

THE MADE-FROM-SCRATCH LIFE

Copyright © 2016 Melissa K. Norris
Published by Harvest House Publishers
Eugene, Oregon 97402
www.harvesthousepublishers.com

Library of Congress Cataloging-in-Publication Data
Norris, Melissa K., 1981-
The made-from-scratch life / Melissa K. Norris.
    pages cm
Includes index.
ISBN 978-0-7369-6534-7 (pbk.)
ISBN 978-0-7369-6535-4 (eBook)
1. Home economics. 2. Home—Religious aspects—Christianity. I. Title.
TX147.N825 2016
640—dc23
                                                    2015021173

Printed in the United States of America

16 17 18 19 20 21 22 23 24 / BP-JH / 10 9 8 7 6 5 4 3 2

To my husband,
who has fully embraced this way of life
and my forays into making everything from scratch
(even the flops),
and supported my dream of being a writer
when I didn't believe in myself.
This wouldn't be possible without you.

Contents

Grow

Remain in me, as I also remain in you. No branch can
bear fruit by itself; it must remain in the vine. Neither can
you bear fruit unless you remain in me. I am the vine; you
are the branches. If you remain in me and I in you, you
will bear much fruit; apart from me you can do nothing.

JOHN 15:4-5

*Growing your own food is rewarding on so many levels. I think
everyone should try to grow some of their own food. You may not
have been born into a gardening family, but I promise you, you can
become a gardener. Of course, there's a learning curve and there
might be frustrations along the way. In fact, if you don't run into
some sort of conundrum I'd be surprised. Anything worth doing
will make you forge on ahead and over problems, and gardening is
no different. This chapter contains my best tips for helping to curb
those pitfalls as much as possible. Like anything in life, you'll continue to learn more every year you garden.*

*Each area and climate zone will have its own unique challenges
and requirements. We won't cover everything here that you may
come up against, but this will give you a good base and hopefully
highlight areas for seasoned gardeners to look at as well.*

Varying shades of green and brown, like a crocheted afghan, lay out before me. Birds twittered. Our chickens scratched the spring grass, searching for a tasty bite. All seemed normal in our small section of the foothills.

Two days before, a devastating landslide had ripped through one of our neighboring communities. Homes were swept away, lives ended, loved ones went missing among the old-growth trees that toppled and snapped like toothpicks in mud.

We live in a small mountain town, though by saying *town*, I'm being generous. We have a post office, a gas station, and a bar. That's it. The nearest stoplight is 40-plus miles away. And we like it that way, we really do.

A volunteer fire department also serves as our ambulance crew and emergency medical technicians. They respond to every emergency in our area—medical, fire, or anything else. My husband is one of those volunteers and an EMT.

Saturday morning his pager went off. We were in the middle of pruning our grapevines, but we're used to the interruption of the beep and static from his pager, followed by a message explaining the situation. When he left, I never dreamed what he would face or what would unfold in the following days.

The report came in of a mudslide covering the highway. Apparently there was a roof in the middle of the road. We'd had a mudslide take out our power and close the highway down about five years ago. I envisioned the same sort of thing.

This wasn't the case. Upon arrival, a sea of mud over 16 feet deep covered the road and valley. The mountain had been sheared off, leaving a gaping wound of raw dirt. Homes were jumbled among the wreckage. People were buried beneath the broken mountainside.

My husband and his team were some of the first ones in on the east side of the slide. In order to keep above the mudflow and avoid need-ing rescuing themselves, they had to step on logs or other bits of debris.

For two hours they rescued and recovered people from the ruins. Then the slide became too unstable, and officials evacuated them from the area they were working.

News started trickling in about the severity of the slide. We could only get snippets of details. This was no small mudslide. Almost half of the mountain had slid. Waves of mud, logs, trees, and water over a square mile wide slammed into more than 50 homes. In places, it was over 20 feet deep. The landslide was so large, it actually stopped the river. Talk of flash flooding and evacuations began.

People were being pulled from the wreckage and airlifted to hospi-tals. Reports of a baby and child being rescued filtered through.

I tried to leave the computer, to go about our day, but like a humming-bird to syrup, I couldn't stop checking the news. The only prayer I could push out was a sporadic, "Jesus, please be with these people. Help them."

The phone rang. It was my husband, and I gripped the phone. "How is it?"

"Not good. The river is backing up, and the area's not stable. They're evacuating us from this area of the slide. I don't know if I'll be home tonight. Don't hold dinner; put the chickens up. My phone battery is dying. I love you."

"I love you. Be careful."

He disconnected.

I sat there for a moment, unable to put down the phone. What was happening? Were the rescuers safe? Not only was my husband on the rescue team, but my neighbors, people I grew up with, lifelong friends.

My children asked when their father was coming home. They know when Daddy is out on a call, he's gone to help someone, but these calls usually last no more than a few hours. It had already been five.

What should I tell them? How much should I share? The urge to gloss it over tempted me, but the need to be honest was bigger.

"There was a big mudslide, and Daddy went to help pull people out of it. It's really large, and a lot of people need help."

My four-year-old stared at me. "Then we should pray to Jesus."

Her words rippled over me. I'd been worried about how they would react, but evidence of the faith I prayed would grow in them shone through like the August sun. "You're right. We should."

My children and I held hands, a small circle of three in our living room, and we prayed out loud. We prayed for safety, for guidance, and for protection. They went back outside to play.

I stood in the living room, staring at where we'd prayed together. Of all the lessons I teach my children, I pray the ones of faith will be the ones that stick. My goal is to be an example, to lift them up and encourage them. On this day, in this moment, it was they who lifted me up. They showed me at their tender ages they already know what to do in a crisis. Pray.

Prayer is such a simple act. It's one we often forget to lead with. But the older I get, the more I realize the simple things are usually the most powerful.

The day wore on. I found myself checking the news updates online more often than I should. My heart dropped to the floor.

They'd lost contact with one of the rescue crews.

My legs shook. I called my husband's phone. Straight to voicemail. My throat tightened. False alarm, the crew was fine. Words of sweet relief on the screen.

I collapsed into my computer chair. He was safe. My husband was safe. But so many other wives' husbands weren't. They were buried in the mud.

Tears burned. The enormity crashed over me. *Jesus.* The only name I could utter. *Be with them, be with us.*

Supper came and went. I managed to get the spaghetti on the table and the kids fed. Bedtime rolled around.

I sat in my chair in the living room. My throat swelled. The television played, but my mind refused to focus long enough to watch. I eyed the clock. Would he come home tonight?

Seconds ticked by, turning into minutes. Grit filled my eyes. I forced myself to swallow past the permanent lump lodged in my throat.

Quarter to eleven. I pushed myself up from the chair. My fingers hovered over the porch light switch. Best to leave it on.

And then the familiar sound of our truck's engine.

Headlights illuminated our yard. I waited, listening to the sound of his boots up the back steps. He entered the house. Dried swipes of dirt and mud darkened his jaw. His eyes spoke a terrible story.

He told me what he'd gone through, what they'd seen, what they'd done. I sat in the chair across from him and wept. I couldn't speak. There were no words anyway. I listened.

I'm a fixer, a doer, a roll-my-sleeves-up-and-get-in-there kind of person. But there are times when I can't do anything. In these times I learn to lean on God. Because when I can't do anything, I step back and let Him take over.

I finally went to bed, spent from the events.

The next day was Sunday. Though I always look forward to our church service, I craved it this morning. I needed to feel the presence of Jesus.

During the church service, I felt the sweet comfort of my Savior in the worship music, felt the wash of peace when we read His words from the Bible. But by the time I returned home, sorrow and anxiety had wedged themselves between my shoulder blades. The news coverage showed nothing but pictures and reports of the slide.

As the day wore on, my nerves stretched taut like the skin on an overripe tomato. I turned off the computer and television, and stepped outside. Two days before, I'd purchased some new herbs and flowers for the whiskey barrel planters flanking our front door. Trowel in hand, I sank down beside the planters.

***

Unable to draw nutrients from the ground, containers need some type of plant food or organic matter added to the soil each year. In the same way, we're unable to draw from our Savior when we're not in direct contact with Him.

Not bothering with gloves, I added a layer of compost to the planters. After I freed the plants from their plastic containers, I broke up the roots from their bound mass before placing them in their spots. Dirt caked my fingers. Silvery green sage leaves greeted me. Bright mint leaves promised fragrance for months to come and fresh flavor for drinks and teas.

With my hands covered in soil, I felt Jesus say, *I bring new life. I am the giver of new beginnings. Death cannot win; I have conquered it. And I will bring newness and healing to this as well.*

Tears of thankfulness warmed my eyes. I closed them and let the warmth of His promise and the afternoon sun soak into my skin. As He cares for the birds and the lilies of the field, how much more does He care for us?

While God has met me in many places, I feel a special nearness to Him when I'm working in my garden. I'm reminded that when things are bleak and dark, He is already at work beneath the dormancy, preparing new seeds and new growth for the right time. He is our master gardener. And our lives closely resemble the seasons of nature. We must pass through each season before we can enter the next.

* * *

My family has been saving and passing down our own strain of green pole bean for over a hundred years, near as we can trace.

When my father was five years old, he and my grandparents migrated from the Appalachian mountains of North Carolina to the steep slopes of the Pacific Northwest. My grandfather was a logger, and during the years of the Great Depression, jobs in the hollers of North Carolina were few. Reliable work wasn't something to take for granted.

My grandfather and two other men converted the back of an old truck into a flatbed with walls, a roof, a stove, and bunk beds. Two small windows allowed light to shine through the homemade camper.

Three families made the trip out west. They shared the back of the wooden camper, ten kids and six adults with all their belongings. A cast-iron skillet, a few pots, and some tin plates were packed to do the cooking. Most people were lucky if they had more than two to three changes of clothes. A large suitcase held the whole family's wardrobe and fit underneath one of the bunk beds. Bigger items were tied to the roof of the truck. Ropes lashed the necessities to the outside walls of the camper.

Soon the mountains and trees of North Carolina grew distant. The roads were no longer familiar.

They could only pack so much food. When they hit the prairie states, they'd run out of bread. When we go to the store, a typical treat is ice cream, a gourmet chocolate, or perhaps an iced coffee with syrup and whipped cream on top. But my father vividly remembers stopping at a general store on their road trip and buying a loaf of white Wonder Bread. Store-bought bread was a treat, and one rarely indulged in.

They found a place to pull off alongside the road, the sea of grass a flat, endless ocean rolling before them. Soft bread lathered with butter was an extravagance greater than any French croissant. He was five years old, and of all the experiences they had on the trip west, this is one that's stuck with him over the decades.

* * *

Would you consider a simple piece of bread a special treat? But how much better would our lives be if we did consider the small, ordinary things as special? It's one of my goals in life to stop and thank God for the things I normally take for granted. Try it and see if it doesn't change your overall outlook on life.

It took a little over a week of travel to make it to Washington. My grandfather found work in the woods as a logger. The mountains were full of large timber. If you've ever viewed the vast slopes of the North Cascade mountain range, you'd be amazed to think that men with a couple of handsaws could harvest trees twenty feet thick and hundreds of feet tall.

My grandmother set about making their home with the meager supplies they'd brought west with them. Tucked into those belongings was a small seed, just as big as your fingernail, white and smooth. But from this one small seed God created enough food to feed their family through the winter months. From this one seed, God created enough food to feed uncountable families for decades to come.

The seed was that of a Tarheel green pole bean. These green beans are a heritage (or heirloom) bean. At the time of my grandparents' migration, there wasn't such a thing as hybrid seed on the market yet. Genetically modified foods weren't something anyone would have fathomed.

This is beautiful to me. The seed doesn't cost a thing. When planted it produces enough food to feed your family, and as it dies it provides you with the means to do it all over again. You see, God knew what He was doing when He created this world. Nature was made to work in balance. It's when we mess with it that things get off-kilter.

* * *

Heirloom seeds are exactly as God created them when He made the world. They haven't been touched by scientists or manipulated like store-bought hybrid seeds, which are sterile, or like genetically modified seeds, which I believe can cause much harm to your health and our natural ecosystem.

Heirloom Vegetables

Of all the information I could share about gardening, my greatest desire is to tell people about using and growing heirloom plants. The vastness of variety and flavor is beyond anything you're used to finding on your grocery store shelf or in the small set of hybrid seed packets for sale in many stores. They're the only seed you can save every year and have it grow back.

When my husband and I were first dating, he came to my parents' house for dinner. We'd been dating long enough that I knew he didn't like green beans. But it was his first time having a meal at my parents' home. It was summertime and my mother had cooked up a big pot of our Tarheel green beans. When I saw him dish up some of the beans, I knew he didn't want to offend my mother by not eating what she'd prepared.

When my mother got up to get dessert, he reached for the pot of green beans. I thought he was really trying to impress my parents. I whispered, "I know you don't like green beans. It's okay; you don't have to take seconds. My mom won't care."

He plopped a large spoonful on his plate. "I don't like green beans, but I love these."

Every spring of our marriage we have planted and grown these beans. My children won't eat green beans from the store or in a restaurant. They can taste the difference. So can I.

I've never found our variety of green beans in the store or seed catalogs. I've had people contact me over the years who haven't saved their seed and are eagerly seeking them out, or who have heard of the beans and want to try them. I'm sure my grandparents never imagined the reach this seed would have when they packed it with them.

When I think about what God can do with one small seed, I think about how much more He can do with my life if I allow Him to be the gardener of my heart. No matter what condition your garden is in, or the season, God is preparing you for the next. I hope your garden grows with the rain of God's forgiveness and the sun of His love.

Making Your Garden from Scratch

Learning to grow a garden is one of the most rewarding things my family and I do. We are able to cut back on our food bill, eat healthier, become more self-sustainable, teach our children a strong work ethic, and observe the incredible way God created nature to work in rhythm.

Did you know that food grown at home has more nutrients and vitamins than produce bought at the store, farmers' markets, or even

Community Supported Agriculture (CSA) programs? When food is allowed to ripen on the vine, it develops more nutrients and vitamins than early-harvested crops. Once it's picked, it begins to lose those nutrients and vitamins.

Food we purchase in the store is picked before it's fully ripe to allow for shipping time and the time it sits out on the shelf. It doesn't have a chance to fully develop its nutrients. Although farmers' markets are local and don't require as much shipping time, they still take some. CSAs usually deliver once a week during the harvest months, but even then, you won't be eating food straight from the vine.

When you grow your food at home, you pick it and prepare it immediately. No time for it to lose its nutrients and vitamins. It's also amazing to taste the difference between vine-ripened, just-picked food and vegetables that have been shipped halfway across the country or world.

Some of you may be thinking, *I don't have enough acreage or a huge yard to grow a big garden.* That's okay. Even if all you have is a windowsill, you can still grow some of your own food. Even if you don't own any land or don't have any yard space, many communities are now offering up gardening space in a community garden. You can also do container gardening on a patio, porch, or deck. You can plant a small windowsill herb garden.

The first thing you need to do is commit to gardening for at least one season. Deciding to do something, instead of just thinking about it, is half the battle. Enlist the help of your family and make it something you all do together.

Choosing Your Garden Site

Choose your garden spot wisely.

You'll want to make sure the place you choose has adequate sunlight. Most plants require at least six hours of sunlight. Shade-tolerant plants—greens and short-season crops like radishes—will usually perform with less sunlight while your tomatoes and peppers will require more. Most fruit and vegetables will do best with full sun. When choosing your site, remember that trees that are bare in winter will provide more shade when their leaves come out in spring and summer. Tall buildings will cast less shade in the summer months when the angle of the sun is higher.

Consider how close you are to your water supply. If you're carrying water by hand you don't want to haul it too far. If using sprinklers or drip hoses, you don't want to have to run miles of hoses or have to move them every time you mow the lawn.

Look at the slope of the ground. In a heavy rainstorm, will all the water run down and pool in your garden spot? A level area is preferable so you don't have water pooling. Look for natural windbreaks if possible. Windy sites can batter tender or tall plants, will dry the plants and soil, and can also cause erosion.

Avoiding some of these pitfalls will make your gardening easier. Remember, though, that there are ways to make a garden work on some level no matter what your conditions are. If you lack the perfect spot, don't let it deter you from putting in a garden. Work with what you have.

Soil and Compost

After choosing your garden spot, you'll want to look at your soil. Is it sandy, rocky, or primarily clay? Does it drain well? Knowing what kind of soil you have will help you know how to amend it. Most soil will benefit from the addition of some good organic matter. Your plants are living things and need good food in order to grow and produce. This can be from a compost pile, aged and dried-out manure (not fresh), or even fertilizer purchased from the store. Seed meal, feather meal, and bagged manure make good fertilizer to grow healthy plants.

Manure from any animal will work. Chicken, cow, horse, and llama or alpaca manure is most common. The key is to turn and cover the manure. If used when fresh, the seed of whatever the animal has been eating may begin to grow in your garden area. Fresh manure is oftentimes too hot or has too much nitrogen in it, and it can kill your plants if applied directly to the roots. Mix the manure with some straw or sawdust, cover it, and allow it to sit for a few months before applying it to your garden. This works especially well if done in the fall (hot weather can make the smell a bit more unpleasant), and by the time spring planting comes around, it will be ready to be mixed into the soil.

* * *

The heat from composting microbes working to decompose the organic material is what kills the weed seeds. To make sure this happens, you'll need the right ratio of carbon and nitrogen. The best ratio for a beginning compost pile is 30 parts carbon to 1 part nitrogen. Carbon materials are often referred to as *brown* and include wood chips, dry leaves, cardboard, and branches. Nitrogen materials are referred to as *greens* and include grass clippings, manure from cattle, sheep, goats, and chickens, and fruit and vegetable scraps. It is not advised to use dairy, meat, or fat scraps as these can attract unwanted pests.

Keeping this pile moist and turning it often will help keep temperatures high enough to kill the weed seeds. Your soil will also benefit from the addition of seed meal and even alfalfa hay.

While the pH level of your soil is important and we're going to discuss it a little bit here, it's not as important as having well fed soil. Most plants will still grow in soil that leans slightly one way or the other—acidic or alkaline. For example, we successfully grew broccoli, cabbage, and brussels sprouts in our acidic soil long before I knew they preferred a more neutral pH of 6.5.

However, knowing the acidity level of your soil can help you troubleshoot and grow a more successful garden. Living in the Pacific Northwest, our soil is generally on the slightly acidic side. This works well for blueberries, raspberries, and potatoes, as well as most vegetables. However, beets and brassicas like more neutral soil.

* * *

There are lots of at-home soil test kits, and most county extension offices will test it for you as well. An easy way to judge the acidity of your soil is by the color of blossoms of a hydrangea bush. If the blossoms are blue your soil is acidic. If they're more pink, your soil is alkaline.

To amend acidic soil you can add wood ash or lime. If it's too alkaline and you need to raise the acidity level, you can use sulfur or coffee grounds. Some studies show used coffee grounds to have a medium level of acidity, while others put them at only slightly acidic. Any time you're amending your soil you'll want to start with a small amount. You can always add more, but you can't take it back out.

Choosing What to Plant

My best advice when gardening is not to start out too big. It's easy to go through seed catalogs and walk through the produce aisles of the grocery store dreaming about growing all you see there on your own. Most of us would love to cut back on our grocery bill, and growing your own food certainly does help with that. When we're plunking in seedlings or seeds, it doesn't look like all that much. But when all of those plants start to grow and require more care, you'll begin to wonder what on earth you were thinking.

Start by planting what you and your family eat a lot of and grows well for your region. For example, here in the Pacific Northwest I can't successfully grow okra, sweet potatoes, or peanuts. The weather simply isn't hot enough for those plants. Peppers and tomatoes tend to do the best with a greenhouse here, though they can be grown outdoors (depending upon the summer). Peppers and tomatoes will flourish for those in the south or hotter areas, but beets and snow peas might not fare as well.

Most seed catalogs and seed packets will specify an ideal region or climate zone. Getting advice from someone who has gardened successfully in your region is important. They will know from experience and be able to guide you. You can also get a lot of advice from a local independent nursery. They've been quite helpful when we were trying to decide which varieties of apple trees and strawberries to put in. Many of them will also have seedlings of vegetables known to do well in your specific zone and region.

Another way we select what to plant is by how well the item can be preserved. While cucumbers are most people's go-to for pickling, my family really doesn't care for cucumber pickles. However, we've been known to eat an entire quart of pickled asparagus at one meal. We only grow one hill of cucumbers for fresh eating on salads and focus on putting in more beans for dilly beans and regular canned green beans. Some lettuce is planted as we like fresh salads, but unless you're using it in a green smoothie, frozen lettuce isn't that appealing or versatile. Instead, we like to grow kale or spinach, both of which can be frozen and used in different dishes.

Each family is unique and it's important to remember to tailor what you grow in accordance with what your family prefers. Don't worry about starting out small either, thinking it won't be enough. Being able to stay on top of a small garden will have you eager to plant more next year. Every year we bring in one new vegetable or variety to try. Usually that means we end up enlarging our garden plot bit by bit as well. Working new ground and just planting cover crops the first year is a great way to get your soil ready for new vegetables. It helps reduce the weeds, lets old sod break down, and builds organic matter. There are lots of reasons to expand slowly.

Container Gardening

If your soil is clay or not in good shape, many people prefer to put in raised beds or to use large containers. This also works well if you don't have very much land. Even people with a back deck or small patio can do container gardening.

It's important to ensure that the container is large enough to support the root system of whatever you're planting. Make sure there are ample drain holes in the bottom of the container as well as some drainage material, such as rock or gravel, with the soil on top. You don't have to invest in fancy containers if you don't want to. Five-gallon food-safe buckets work well, and many times you can get them free from a local restaurant or bakery.

You can purchase bags of potting soil for your containers in the gardening section of almost any store. Our local nursery carries large bags of organic potting mix. I personally would look for potting soil that doesn't have synthetic fertilizers added to it. If you need to bring in a lot of soil, you may want to contact a large landscaper in your area, explain to them what you're after, and have it delivered in a dump truck.

Buying Seeds

So you've got your garden spot picked out and figured out whether you need to amend your soil. Now it's time to pick your seeds! We only grow foods from heirloom seeds—some of those varieties being ones my family has saved for generations. But how can you ensure you're getting good quality heirloom seeds?

Most grocery stores don't carry a large variety of heirloom seeds, if any. There's nothing wrong with planting hybrid seeds, but I prefer the heirloom seed for their history, flavor, variety, and the assurance they're not genetically modified. I like to work with companies that preserve varieties and strains that, once gone, are lost forever.

Planting

It's time to plant! Putting the seeds in the garden is one of my favorite things. That simple action holds such promise and hope and reminds me of how God plants little seeds in our lives that later grow into full-fledged beautiful blessings.

There are two ways to plant your garden, depending on what you want to plant. One is to use transplants or seedlings, and the other is direct sowing. Direct sowing is simply putting the seed into the ground. Transplants and seedlings can either be purchased from a nursery or local gardening store or grown and nurtured inside your home.

Transplants and seedlings can extend the growing season for those of us living in an area with a shorter or cooler summer. Tomatoes and peppers are two plants I have to start indoors or purchase seedlings for. You can even transplant sweet corn and snap peas to give you a thicker stand and a jump on the season.

You'll also see seedlings for most winter and summer squash. We typically put our direct-sow seeds in the ground the last part of May. Our growing season for warm-weather plants ends in September. This barely gives us four months.

I have grown seedlings for winter and summer squash but have found direct sown seeds to perform better. No matter how much care you use when transplanting the seedlings, it takes them a while to recover from the transplant and really start growing. The plants I've direct sown grow just as quickly as the transplants and many times outgrow them due to not having to recover from the transplant. Some plants, like beans, don't respond to being transplanted at all and should be directly sown.

The success of your plants and harvest will rely on your putting your seeds or transplants into the ground at the right time. You need to know your area's average first and last frost date. You'll want to avoid putting out seedlings and the seeds of warm-weather plants until all danger of frost has passed. Vegetables that can be planted during the cooler months are spinach, lettuce, carrots, beets, cabbage, kale, broccoli, snow peas, and brussels sprouts. All types of squash, green beans, peppers, corn, and tomatoes require warm soil (over 65 degrees) and need to be planted after all danger of frost. To find your area's average first and last frost dates, you can do a simple Internet search or ask an experienced gardener in your area. Many local or independent nurseries also have this information.

Below is a full list of how early to start seedlings indoors and a chart of which plants to direct sow and when. Write in your sow date after researching the dates of your first and last frost. (When the "start indoors" column is left blank, this indicates that the plants will, generally speaking, perform better when direct sown.)

Plant	Start Indoors	Plant Outside	My Sow Date
Beans, pole and bush		3-4 weeks after last spring frost	
Beans, shell-ies or dry		3-4 weeks after last spring frost	
Beets		2-4 weeks before last spring frost *or* 4 weeks before first fall frost	
Broccoli	7 weeks before last spring frost	2 weeks before last spring frost	
Cabbage	6 weeks before last spring frost	2 weeks before last spring frost, or direct sow in mid to late summer for a fall crop	
Carrots		2-4 weeks before last spring frost. Can continue to sow up until 8 weeks before first fall frost.	
Cauliflower	8 to 10 weeks before last spring frost	2 weeks before last spring frost	
Chard	4 weeks before last spring frost	On last spring frost date *or* 6-12 weeks before first fall frost	
Corn		2-4 weeks after last spring frost	

Plant	Start Indoors	Plant Outside	My Sow Date
Cucumbers	On last spring frost date	3-4 weeks after last spring frost	
Garlic		6-8 weeks before first fall frost	
Kale		4-6 weeks before last spring frost *or* 2-3 weeks before first fall frost	
Lettuce		4 weeks before last spring frost. Sow every 2-3 weeks for continual harvest.	
Onions	10-16 weeks before last spring frost	6 weeks before to 4 weeks after last spring frost	
Parsnips		2 weeks before last spring frost	
Peas	8 weeks before last spring frost	4-6 weeks before last spring frost	
Peppers	4-8 weeks before last spring frost (8 weeks for cooler climates)	3-4 weeks after last spring frost	
Potatoes		2-4 weeks before last spring frost to as late as 2-3 weeks after last spring frost	
Rutabaga		4-6 weeks before last spring frost	

Plant	Start Indoors	Plant Outside	My Sow Date
Spinach		6 weeks before last spring frost *or* 8 weeks before first fall frost	
Squash, summer	2 weeks before last spring frost	2-4 weeks after last spring frost	
Squash, winter/ pumpkin	2 weeks before last spring frost	2-4 weeks after last spring frost	
Tomatoes	2-8 weeks before last spring frost		
Turnips		2-4 weeks before last spring frost	
Watermelon	On last spring frost date	4 weeks after last spring frost	

In order to speed up the germination time (the time between planting the seed and seeing it sprout), we soak some of our seeds the night before planting. This helps shorten the germination time by at least a few days. I've had much higher success rates with my beet and bean seeds by soaking them. Just place them in a bowl of room temperature water overnight. In the morning, drain and plant your seeds. I don't soak tiny seeds, like tomatoes, peppers, carrots, lettuce, or spinach. Primarily, we just soak the beet, bean, and corn seed.

* * *

Check the forecast during planting week as you don't want to put your seeds in the ground if a huge rainstorm is on its way. One, it can wash the seed away if really heavy, and two, if the ground is too saturated, the seeds may rot.

When planting your garden, use the height of your plants to your advantage. Tomatoes, peppers, beans, and corn prefer full sun. Lettuce, spinach, and snow peas can tolerate cooler temperatures. Our beans are a pole bean, so they get to be about four feet tall. I'll plant our lettuce on the back side of taller plants so the plants don't get the full force of the midday sun. On the other hand, you wouldn't want to plant your corn in the front of the garden where it would keep all of the plants in the shade.

Six Tips on Planting Beans

1. **Direct sow your beans.** Beans do not grow well as seedlings or transplants. They are best sowed directly into the ground as a seed. Beans should be sown when the soil temperature (not the air temperature) is at least 60 degrees Fahrenheit.

2. **Soak your beans overnight.** The night before you plant your beans, soak the seeds in room temperature water overnight. This will greatly speed up the germination process. However, if the weatherman foretells rain for your region during your bean-planting week, don't soak the seeds because they could rot.

3. **Plant your beans where your brassicas were planted the previous year.** Beans are an excellent plant when it comes to crop rotation because they help fix nitrogen in the soil. It's a good idea to plant them where members of the brassica family (cabbage, broccoli, Brussels sprouts, or cauliflower) were planted the previous year.

4. **Take advantage of companion planting.** Beans are a fairly non-picky plant and get along nicely with almost everything else. The only plants you shouldn't plant in their vicinity are members of the allium family, like onions, garlic, leek, and scallions. The allium family can inhibit or stunt the growth of green beans.

5. **Run a string over your planted bean seeds.** Birds are notorious for pulling up new bean sprouts. If you tie a string just an inch or two over the row of sprouts, it prevents the birds from pulling them up. After the beans are a few inches tall, you can remove the string.

6. **Know if the beans are a bush or pole variety.** The seed package

should tell you if it's a pole or bush variety. Bush beans don't need a support system and are rather bushy and lower to the ground. Pole beans send up vine runners and need something to climb. You can use a pole, fencing, or even run strands of string or wire between two poles to create a trellis system. Once the runners begin to grow, you need to get the plants something to climb on. They won't grow if they don't have their support system. After putting your climbing supports in place, the beans literally grow inches overnight. Our bean is a pole variety and quite prolific.

How to Plant Potatoes

1. **Only plant seed potatoes.** Potatoes you've purchased in the grocery store are not suitable for seed potatoes because they haven't been harvested that way. They also may have been sprayed with chemicals to keep them from sprouting on the shelf. Seed potatoes are chosen for their resistance to disease. I know some people do plant potatoes they've purchased from the store once they've sprouted, but I'd rather not take the gamble of introducing any disease to my soil.

2. **Choose acidic soil that drains well and has been fertilized.** Potatoes are heavy feeders. You don't want them to rot in the ground or develop a fungus. Never plant where you had tomatoes the previous year. Always rotate your potatoes each year.

3. **Potatoes prefer cooler weather**, and they can be put in the ground as early as two weeks before your last frost date. They'll tolerate some heat, but if temps stay in the 90s or above for prolonged periods of time, they may die.

4. **Dig a trench about 4 to 6 inches deep.** Set the cut potato inside with the eye facing upward. Space 12 inches apart and cover with 2 inches of soil. After potatoes have sprouted, you'll need to mound soil around them.

5. **Know when to mound your potato plants.** Potatoes are produced from the tubers, and if left exposed to light, they'll turn green and poisonous. (Yes, this is true.) Mounding also helps inhibit blight. Mound the soil up once the foliage has reached about 8 inches high

with a hoe. It's better to not mound the soil too steep, so it won't wash away in the rain. Mound up until only 2 inches of leaves are left showing.

6. Additional mounding of dirt should be done once you have new growth of about 4 to 6 inches. This will be repeated 3 to 4 times throughout the growing season. If you don't have the garden space for potatoes, they make an excellent container crop. You simply fill with more dirt instead of mounding each time. I've seen pictures of people using large plastic laundry baskets!

Crop Rotation

After your garden is up and you can identify the plants by their leaves, take a picture. This will help you remember where everything was located next year when you go to plant. Trust me; your memory might not be quite as sharp as you think when you try to recall exactly where everything was a year later. The picture will prove invaluable and help you plot out your crop rotation.

Crop rotation is simply planting your plants in a different spot from the previous year. Different plants take different amounts of nutrients from the soil. Rotating them by plant family and whether the harvested portion is roots, leaves, or flowers will help keep your soil balanced and reduce the threat of insects and disease. By practicing crop rotation, you will reduce your risk of many soil-borne viruses and other soil problems that can negatively affect your plants.

There are two plant families that especially require crop rotation: solanaceae and brassicas.

The solanaceae family includes nightshade plants like tomatoes, peppers, and potatoes. These are all susceptible to the same pests and diseases. You don't want to plant these plants in the same spot or soil where any related plants have grown in the past three years. This is why it is also important to purchase certified seed potatoes when planting, as you can unknowingly introduce viruses to your soil otherwise.

The brassica family, sometimes referred to as cruciferous vegetables, includes broccoli, cabbage, Brussels sprouts, and cauliflower. Brassicas like nitrogen-rich soil. Legumes (beans and peas) will put nitrogen back into your soil through their roots, so planting brassicas where you had beans or peas the year prior is a good idea. As with the solanaceae vegetables, don't plant brassicas in a space where related plants have grown in the previous three years.

Weeds

Let's talk about weeds. There are many different trains of thoughts when it comes to weeds in the garden. Some weeds are in fact edible, but you want to make sure you have a really good reference manual before pulling up and eating something without knowing exactly what it is—and what side effects it might cause.

* * *

Dandelions are widely considered an annoying weed. However, dandelions can be harvested and all parts of the plant are edible. Use caution when picking from anywhere the plants may have been sprayed or by busy roadways due to pollution. The greens are best when picked young in the spring so they're not bitter. They can be added to salads, steamed, or added to soups or casseroles. Some people even dry and grind them up for coffee substitutes. I've seen the blossoms dipped in batter and fried.

Dandelions have many vitamins and minerals and most of us walk over them every spring and summer, never thinking about a free food supply. We so often look at things as a nuisance or annoyance when really, they can be gifts. The changing of perspective is a wonderful thing. Instead of an annoying weed the dandelion may be your next culinary masterpiece...or at the very least a way to lower the cost of your food bill.

There are basically two methods to weed control in the vegetable garden. I say two because we don't use chemical pesticides as a manner of weed control on our food, and I don't recommend it for anyone else. So it's either pull them up or smother them. There are advantages to both methods and you'll have to experiment and decide which works best for you and your garden.

The best way to manage weeds is a three-step process.

1. Use stakes and string to lay out rows. Plant your seeds on a straight line and leave the string in place. (This also keeps birds from pulling up your young seedlings.)

2. Water gently as necessary, avoiding too much cold water.

3. In seven to ten days, depending on the temperature, come back with a *sharp* (shallow is best) hoe and gently scrape or stir the top inch around, avoiding the planted line. If you look carefully, you'll see the threadlike roots of the emerging weed seeds, and you'll see that you've just killed most of the problem in less than five minutes. Timing is everything!

Of course, the most basic method is to simply pull up the weeds by hand when you see them. This takes time and if you skip a few days—or a week or two—the weeds can quickly overtake your garden. We're normally fairly diligent, but this happened to us last year. While the weeds can steal nutrients from your plants, if left to mature, they'll also go to seed and create even more weeds the following year. Another bad thing is we have poisonous nightshade that grows in our region. We discovered some of those weeds growing were nightshade berries. Yikes!

We donned gloves and pulled and bagged all of the nightshade plants to avoid more reseeding. It was also a time to remind our kids to only pick berries and plants they knew were safe. I learned an important lesson: Stay on top of the weeds. Gardens always provide ample lessons, it seems: Avoiding your problems doesn't make them go away and usually only makes them worse.

If you dedicate 15 minutes a day to hoeing young weeds, you'll stay on top of them. While I can't put in an hour or even a half hour every day, I can always find 15 minutes. Make a plan to put in 15 minutes weeding every day and see how much you can get done. You may go over that, but if you do just the 15 minutes, you'll have accomplished quite a bit when you add it up at the end of the week.

If you've let your weeds go and need a restart, rototill between your rows to put the weeds back into the soil and knock them down. Of course, if you wait until they're going to seed, you're simply replanting more weeds. You don't want to rototill too often as you'll loosen up the soil so much it could damage the roots of your vegetables.

The other method of weed control is to smother them in mulch. This is often referred to as lasagna or permaculture gardening. You keep the soil covered with organic matter—layers of hay, straw, wood chips, and mulch. I personally haven't used this method in our main vegetable garden. I do use woodchip mulch on my blueberry and raspberry plants. They thrive with a good, thick layer of sawdust mixed with manure.

* * *

Use caution if using all wood as your mulch. Wood needs time and nitrogen to break down, and if you incorporate undecomposed wood into your garden, it will use up all the available nitrogen. There won't be any nitrogen left for your vegetables and they will grow poorly. Remember, whatever you put on top of your soil will break down eventually and can change the pH.

A great mulch is your lawn clippings. It's a good reason to have a lawn mower with a catcher. As you mow your lawn you are generating a great weed-free, high nitrogen, easily handled fertilizer/mulch. Lay it one to three inches deep (depending on how big your plants are and how much lawn you have) alongside your berries and vegetables as they grow. If you leave it in piles, it will start cooking and melt, so you need to distribute it as you generate it or within a day or so of mowing.

The mulching method, if done correctly, prevents weeds in two ways. One, it smothers them so they don't have enough light to grow. Second, it provides a protective layer so seeds from new weeds can't reach the soil and take root.

We use the second method in the fall on our garden in the form of either a cover crop or a thick layer of leaves. Instead of leaving our soil bare through the fall and winter months, we place a thick layer of fallen leaves over the dirt. This helps keep it from eroding away during the heavy rains or snow and also keeps any seeds blowing in the wind or from birds flying overhead from being "planted" into our soil. Finally, it provides beneficial nutrients to our garden as it breaks down and is eventually tilled back in come spring.

You can do the same thing with a cover crop. We've used kale as a cover crop, but many popular choices are annual rye grass, buckwheat, and clover. Cover crops should be sown about four to six weeks before your first hard frost.

You've done it. You've decided where to plant, gotten your soil ready, and put in your seedlings. Now what?

Thirsty Plants

You'll want to make sure your garden stays well watered, but not overly so. Soil that drains well will keep plants from drying out too quickly or becoming waterlogged and rotting. Even in the rainy Northwest, we still have to water in the latter part of summer. If you use the mulching method of weed control, you won't have to water as often as the mulch will help keep the moisture in the ground and from evaporating as quickly.

You may wish to use sprinklers, but use care when watering overhead with tomatoes and peppers. Overhead watering with tomatoes can introduce fungus and split the ripe tomatoes. Truly, the best practice is to use drip hoses or water by hand. However, if you have a large garden, watering by hand is going to be too time-consuming. I recommend investing in some soaker hoses.

Soaker hoses are porous and weep water, rather than having it come out the end or spray like a sprinkler system. These are wonderful for areas where mildew or fungus are a problem as they only wet the ground, not the foliage. Because the water comes out slowly, there tends to be less runoff and the ground and roots of the plant get a better soaking (hence the name) than traditional sprinklers or overhead watering systems. They also use less water. One caveat: Don't turn your water on full-force or you can blow out the hose. Keep the pressure down. You can also bury the soaker hoses, but we keep ours aboveground as I move my tomatoes and peppers every year.

The time of day to water is also up for discussion. Never water during the hottest part of the day. You'll shock your plants, plus a lot of the water will evaporate before soaking into the dirt. Some gardeners like to water in the evening as the moisture will stick around longer as the sun won't be up for hours. However, this can introduce mildew or fungus as the water will sit on the plants longer. Other folks prefer to water in the early morning. Your schedule will determine when you water as well. If you leave extremely early in the morning, going outside to water the garden will most likely not happen.

Decide what works best for you and your region. I prefer to water in the morning when I can, but there are times I have to switch it around and water at night. Since we started using the soaker hoses, it doesn't matter as much in regard to morning or evening as the foliage of our plants aren't getting sprayed. We've also had fewer problems with mold and mildew on our plants.

Pest Control

We need to talk a little bit about pest control. Some plants are more naturally inclined to attract and harbor pests than others. Tomatoes are often susceptible to disease, and worms and moths like to bother broccoli. In the southern states, squash is bothered by vine borers. Here we battle with deer who find our garden as tasty as we do.

As with humans, if the plant is healthy from well prepared soil and watering, it will be more likely to withstand an invasion and come through it. Our best protection from deer is good fencing. A good guard dog will also help. (Ours is not. He seems to think the deer make a lovely addition to the landscape.)

Several insects love all members of the cabbage or brassica family. Floating row covers that will keep them from getting to the plants in the first place seems to be the best remedy. A word about row covers: In addition to keeping bugs away from most crops, they hold more heat around the plants. This is especially helpful in the spring or fall when the nights get cold. Row covers can help young seedlings get established and offer protection from the wind. They also keep crows from stealing newly emerging peas and corn.

I have also used organic Neem oil on our potatoes and tomatoes during a flea beetle infestation. Our fruit trees were plagued by a small black aphid, and I used a treatment of Neem oil for them as well. Even with organic methods, make sure to wear proper protective gear, such as long sleeves and pants, gloves, and a mask and gloves when applying treatments. Whenever you're spraying, make sure there's no rain in the forecast and to spray in the morning when there's less chance of a breeze.

* * *

There is little more rewarding than going out to your garden for your first harvest. All of the work and planning are suddenly worth it when you get to eat something grown off of your own land and from the fruits of your labors. Your homegrown food will have more flavor as you harvest it at its peak time, allowing it to fully ripen on the vine and develop all of its flavor and nutrients.

10 Tips for Pest Control

1. Healthy plants are less susceptible to disease and pests. Start with well amended soil to begin with by the addition of compost and cover crops. We use chicken manure to amend our soil. Let chicken manure sit with sawdust or straw for compost. Chicken manure is high in nitrate and too hot to put on your plants fresh. Any manure you put on your plants or in soil should be dry and not fresh. Pig, chicken, llama, horse, and cow manure are likewise excellent sources of natural organic fertilizer.

2. Reuse coffee grounds. Used coffee grounds are an excellent way to add phosphorous, potassium, magnesium, and copper to your soil. It's also slightly acidic. Add a handful to the soil when planting or till it in about six inches deep. Make sure the coffee is spread out and worked into the soil so it doesn't sit in clumps that could mold. Most espresso stands and coffee shops (including Starbucks!) will give you their used coffee grounds for free.

3. Crop rotation. Practicing crop rotation will cut down on many soil-borne viruses and diseases, saving you a lot of angst and time in the garden.

4. Monitor your garden regularly. An early detection of a pest or disease problem will often be the key in successfully eradicating it.

5. Manually remove certain pests. Some pests are easiest to remove by hand. When we had an infestation of flea beetles on our tomato plants, I manually removed them every morning and evening for a week. Spray

aphids with a strong stream of water to dislodge them from plants. You can also get rid of aphids with ladybugs, which can be purchased at garden stores.

6. Diatomaceous Earth (DE). Purchase food grade DE when using on edibles and your vegetable garden. DE is a white powder made from the crushed-up fossilized remains of phytoplankton. When sprinkled on ants, fleas, and mites, it compromises their exoskeletons. It's safe for humans. You can use it to clean chicken coops and to help get rid of mites in your coop. DE is great for beans, broccoli, and cabbage to keep the bugs from crossing the soil to get to the plant. To apply, sprinkle it on the soil surrounding the plant. It's also a much better bet for slugs than salt. Salt kills slugs but also damages your soil.

7. Organic Neem oil (from the African Neem tree). It's best to spray your plants early in the morning. Never spray your plants in the heat of the day (when you could scorch or burn the leaves), at night (when the dew could wash the spray off), or before rain. You should also be careful not to apply it on a windy day; you don't want the spray getting in your face or skin. Neem oil requires two applications about 10 days apart. Be sure to label your spray bottle. Don't save the spray; use it all at once and mix fresh for each application. Anytime you're applying a substance to your plants, use proper safety measures and caution.

8. Row covers or cloth covers. For plants that don't require cross-pollination by bees, using a row or cloth cover in the early spring will keep moths from laying their eggs in the plants.

9. Netting and fencing. Huge pests to our garden and

plants are deer, elk, birds, and occasionally cattle when they wander out of the pasture. Our free-range chickens can also pose a problem to our fruit and vegetable crop. We use netting and fencing to keep the larger pests away. Plastic netting works great on blueberries and raised beds. We protect our garden with metal T-posts and metal fencing. Our young fruit trees have four tall metal T-posts around them, and we use chicken wire and plastic fencing around the main part of the tree and fruit.

10. Watering. Be sure to check your water levels. If the plant is stressed from lack of water, any kind of pest will kill it that much faster. A deep watering once or twice a week is much better than daily watering. Soaker hoses on the tomatoes and peppers overnight provides a much greater benefit than daily watering.

Harvest

The LORD will indeed give what is good,
and our land will yield its harvest.

PSALM 85:12

While there is a joy and lesson to be learned during the planting of things, there is nothing as rewarding as your actual harvest. Plucking sun-ripened food straight from the vine is an experience everyone should have during their life.

The harvest is the reason we keep tending the garden, even when storms ravage and disease runs rampant. We slog through the mess and put in the work, knowing it will all be worth it in the end. The harvest is what will keep you returning to your garden year after year.

Every time I hear someone say tomatoes are one of the easiest plants to grow, my face heats up. My toes curl. My fingers clench into fists. Tomatoes are *not* one of the easiest plants to grow. In fact, they may be one of the hardest. I have tried unsuccessfully for years to grow good large-crop producing tomatoes.

We all have a nemesis in the garden. Mine is tomatoes. Some of you may be saying, "Tomatoes aren't hard to grow; they're super easy. All I do is plop mine in the dirt and I get tons of tomatoes all summer long."

I'm chewing on my tongue right now. I do that when my first reply isn't gracious and kind. My tongue gets chewed on more than I care to admit. If you're one of the above people who have awesome luck with tomatoes, you're hereby required to share your tomato knowledge with the rest of us not-so-great tomato raisers. Or you can just bring us over a bushel of ripe tomatoes.

* * *

There are four pecks in a bushel and each peck is two gallons, so that's eight gallons of tomatoes for a bushel.

I've tried tomatoes in all different ways. We've done the hanging-upside-down method and grown them in raised beds and in pots. We've put them right up against our hot tub in the sunniest spot with the most southern exposure. I've put them underneath the eaves of the house to keep the rainwater off them.

All to no avail.

The ones in pots never went beyond their blossoms. They had tons and tons of blossoms, but no fruit, despite my talking sweetly alternated with a good stern if-you-know-what's-good-for-you warning. The ones hung upside down shriveled up and died. The ones under the eaves of the house developed large black spots of blight all over the fruit before it could ripen. And the ones that didn't develop blight just plain never ripened.

I took the next year off from growing tomatoes. A girl can only handle so many disappointments in a row. But after having to purchase those bushels of tomatoes to can my salsa and stewed tomatoes, the frugal side of me overrode the disappointed side.

Thousands of people grew tomatoes every year. I would join their ranks.

I researched and collected all the tomato-growing tips I could find. My gardener friends answered my numerous questions.

Have you ever noticed how most gardeners are willing to share their knowledge and advice? Get them talking about soil or strains of plants and you may think your feet are going to grow roots before the conversation is over. I think the world would be a better place if we were all willing to share our knowledge. Too often folks are close-fisted, not wanting to give anyone an upper hand or the chance to best them.

Life is not a competition. Though at times I've lived it like it was.

> So the last will be first, and the first will be last
> (Matthew 20:16).

Today's world would have us believe we're going to miss out if we don't keep up. There's a belief we need to come in first, be number one.

This past summer we were camping at a family campground next to a creek. On the weekend they have duck races. You purchase a duck and the winner receives a free pancake breakfast for up to four people.

We heard the call to purchase ducks late as we were playing a family round of mini-golf. Clubs in tow, we hurried over to the desk to purchase our ducks. We barely made the cutoff. There were few ducks to choose from and my daughter had to take the last duck that was available. It was not one of the bright pink ducks already waiting in the basket to be taken down to the creek. She was stuck with one of the plain yellow ducks.

We joined the other families along the shore of the creek at the designated finish line. Anticipation swelled in little bodies and hope shone in faces as they leaned over the edge of the creek, trying to catch a glimpse of the first duck to bob his way downstream. A swarm of ducks flooded the creek.

The first wave of ducks caught in the current and swirled towards the finish line. A few large rocks diverted the stream. The lead duck got stuck behind the rock. Second-place duck washed into an eddy just three feet from the finish line.

Finally, a duck broke free from the pack and wobbled across the finish line to be swept up in the net, the number scrawled in Sharpie across the bottom recorded, and then tucked into the bag. The kids waded out amongst the slippery moss-covered rocks, splashing and giggling as they wrangled the rest of the ducks into a large sack.

With the last stragglers of ducks tied up in the bag, we grabbed our clubs and headed back to finish our round on the golf course. After our game we took the clubs back to the clubhouse. The worker glanced at our daughter. "Did you have a duck in the duck race?"

She nodded her head.

The worker smiled. "I think you were the winner."

My daughter's eyes widened.

The clerk double-checked the records. "Yep, you won the grand prize."

A smile lit up my daughter's face like a full harvest moon. "I won, Mama!"

"Here's your certificate for breakfast tomorrow."

She carried the paper with both hands back to our camper trailer and placed it in the center of the table. "I get to take you guys to breakfast tomorrow."

My husband grinned. "And you were the very last one to pick."

I bent down to her level, dark brown eyes meeting mine. "The Bible says those who go last will be first. Guess this was God's way of showing you." I squeezed her hand. "Of course, sometimes that first won't be here on earth. Sometimes we have to wait until heaven."

The next morning we made our way to the clubhouse to put in our breakfast order. Standing on tiptoe, she slid her certificate over the counter to pay for everyone's breakfast. We approached the kitchen window and when the cook handed over the plates with fluffy syrup-soaked pancakes my daughter met her gaze. "Did you know the Bible says if you go last you'll be first?" Her little voice rang clear across the room.

My mama-heart swelled. We don't always know which seeds we plant will grow and flourish into a harvest when we plant them. But when we get to the harvest time, all of the work, waiting, and wondering is worth it.

I didn't know if my daughter would remember my words from the day before or not. A tiny seed of God between the swimming, scrambling up and down monkey bars, sliding over slippery rocks like a beaver, riding bikes in the last throes of summer, and snuggling into blankets with the faint scent of campfires clinging to our hair, but the biblical words were the ones she remembered the next morning. The words and life lesson I pray she'll continue to harvest for the rest of her life.

When I look at my days and all of the things I try to cram into them, I try to remember the planting and harvesting of God's love is the important part. I want to have the faith of a child. I want to believe without question God is who He says He is. And I want to share it with others, my family, my friends, coworkers, and over a plate of pancakes with a complete stranger.

Another funny thing about us humans is we so often long for a different outcome, but we keep doing the exact same things. If we don't do anything different, we won't receive anything different. Circumstances don't change themselves.

Year after year I struggled with my tomato crop. Year after year I kept planting the tomatoes in the same way but in different spots. Are you noticing a pattern?

For years I went to church. Most of the time. A couple Sundays a month. Or once a month when things were really busy. I wasn't happy with the spiritual harvest I was reaping. Discontentment, uncertainty of my place, restlessness, a searching for more.

If you're unhappy with the harvest you're reaping right now, honestly look at the seeds you've sown. Are you putting God first? Are you spending time going through His Word every day?

When I began reading my Bible on a regular basis at home, it was usually in the evenings. Once the kids and my husband were in bed I'd curl up in the recliner, wrap a blanket around my shoulders, and delve into Scripture. For about five minutes. Then the words blurred. I'd have to reread each verse as my tired mind didn't want to accept one more bit of information.

Sometimes (okay, most times) I nodded off in the chair. This went on for far longer than it should, but we're being honest here, right? Right. Then one day I felt God ask me, "What if I only gave you my tired, leftover minutes?"

Ouch. This got my attention. If God was as important to me as I said, then why was I putting time with Him last?

Conviction made me rise. Bleary-eyed, coffee cup in one hand and my Bible in the other, I padded out to our back deck. Dew blanketed the grass and leaves on the grape arbor. Morning sun streaked the heavens.

Surrounded by God's creation I began to read. His presence washed over me in the breeze ruffling my hair. A half hour easily passed, my coffee grown cold. But I was awake with His Word.

* * *

Remember my nemesis, those tomatoes? They hardly gave me cause to rejoice...until this year. Our harvest remains the same unless we change how we do something. After I questioned people, read countless articles, and changed pretty much everything about the way I raised tomatoes, I reaped my largest harvest ever.

These are things I learned about planting tomatoes. You know, just in case you struggle with them too.

First, tomatoes like to send their roots deep. Small containers, especially those upside-down ones, don't provide enough room for their roots.

Second, the condition of the soil makes all the difference. Tomatoes need calcium to prevent blossom-end rot and lots of good organic matter as they're heavy feeders. Adding crushed up eggshells and a few tablespoons of Epsom salt to the hole when you plant them will help meet their nutritional needs as they grow.

Finally, tomatoes are quite picky about getting their leaves and fruit wet. They don't like to be watered from overhead. For those of you in drier areas of the world, this isn't a problem, but those of us in the Pacific Northwest might as well stick an umbrella over each plant.

And an umbrella was exactly what my tomatoes got! We had an old metal carport frame. The plastic tarp roof had long since rotted and ripped. But a good frame can be transformed into many a useful thing.

I purchased greenhouse plastic and fasteners and repurposed it into one big tomato umbrella, or a cold frame, whichever name you prefer. While frost still kissed the ground, I started my tomato seeds indoors. Every day I'd carefully water them and rotate them underneath the growlight.

When it came time to set my darlings outside I took two weeks to harden off my plants. If you have a plant that's always been kept indoors, you have to gradually let it acclimate and build up a tolerance to the conditions outdoors. The first day you let it sit outside for an hour and then bring it back in. Each day you lengthen the time it is outdoors by an hour or two until you've reached a full 24 hours.

If you don't take this time, your plant will most likely die from shock.

This reminds me of how God matures us. When storms approach, He always provides shelter for us. We might not always choose to take it, but it's always there. As we go through life we'll grow stronger in the Lord, we'll be able to handle bigger storms, and we'll mature...until we set fruit and produce a harvest.

After my tomato plants were in the dirt I wound soaker hoses beneath their base. Not one drop of water was allowed to touch the leaves and tops of my plants. Tomatoes also like to be watered deeply, but less frequently. Instead of daily watering, I turned the hose on twice a week.

Despite all of my prepping and planning I anxiously awaited the first fruits. Clusters of blossoms dotted the vines. In the past, I'd had blossoms but they never formed into tomatoes.

My tomato plants dripped bright green tomatoes. Every day I ventured out into the greenhouse to check on their progress, diligently checking for signs of disease and removing any leaves that were discolored or shriveled. Would they ripen or would blight strike at the last hour?

One morning I walked into the greenhouse. Red tomatoes glistened on the vines like ornaments at Christmas. I may have wept just a little.

We harvested bucket upon bucket of tomatoes. Gorgeous vine-ripened bursting-with-flavor tomatoes.

* * *

One of the main reasons I wanted tomatoes in the first place was to be able to can most of our own tomato products for our pantry shelves. Ever cut into a tomato and had juice seep everywhere?

When you make sauce or salsa, you want it on the thicker side, not a watery soupy mess. And flavor, we want flavor. All this to say you need to plant a paste tomato. Paste tomatoes have less water and thicker flesh. Perfect for salsa and sauce.

Can you use a non-paste tomato? Certainly, but the yield of your recipes won't be as high. The recipes will also take longer to make and won't be as flavorful.

I rejoiced in those tomatoes. We had fried green tomatoes, tomato salsa, and pico de gallo, and the preserving of the harvest began. For years I've wanted to make and can my own tomato sauce, but I never had enough. (You need quite a few tomatoes to make a decent-size batch of sauce, as in 35 pounds.) I waited and waited for there to be enough ripe tomatoes at once. You can also pick the tomatoes as they ripen, blanch them in hot water for a few minutes, skin them, and toss the skinless tomatoes in the freezer until you've amassed enough for a batch of sauce. With my 18 tomato plants, I didn't have to use this method because I had plenty of them ripe at once.

Homemade tomato sauce has so much more flavor than sauce from the store. I was amazed at how sweet it tastes all on its own. After dishing up our first spaghetti made with my homemade sauce my husband said, "This is the best I've ever tasted."

There are many lessons to be learned out in the garden. I completely get why Jesus used so many parables concerning the growing of things.

> A farmer went out to sow his seed. As he was scattering the seed, some fell along the path; it was trampled on, and the birds of the air ate it up. Some fell on rocky ground, and when it came up, the plants withered because they had no moisture. Other seed fell among thorns, which grew up with it and choked the plants. Still other seed fell on good soil. It came up and yielded a crop, a hundred times more than was sown (Luke 8:5-8).

The first thing I notice about this parable is that *the farmer sowed his seed*. We can't expect a harvest in an area we don't plant. But so often we do. We want an organized home, but we don't do the work of making it happen. We want a powerful prayer life, but we don't put in the time of storing God's Word in our heart and praying.

The second thing the parable shows is that we can sow the seed, but if we don't learn to tend it, it will die before it's had a chance to produce a harvest. How many times have I experienced the power of God and vowed to live on fire for Him? I'll bet you have too. When He answers a prayer and spares the life of a loved one or meets a financial need or shows through the tender words of a friend that we are loved, we vow to live our lives devoted to Him.

Then life happens, the daily drudge of work and to-do lists slowly take over, and suddenly, we're not where we wanted to be. But God is a merciful farmer. As soon as we turn back to Him, He brings forth new growth.

Sometimes the seeds we've sown (or that others have sown into our lives) stay dormant. The seed hides out of sight, waiting for us to reach the right conditions before it bursts from the soil of our soul, ready to grow and bear fruit. I love these types of seeds. They are God's way of reminding me He was planning and directing things long before I was even aware of them. It's His gentle and sweet reminder that, "I've got you, daughter. I've always had you, I've always been here, and I always will be. Trust me."

It's important to feed our plants so they can continue to grow. Some require soil imbalances, added organic matter (dried manure works wonders), and monitoring of their water. If we don't feed our souls with time in God's Word and don't spend time in prayer, we will stunt our growth and patches of disease and stress will begin to show.

But when we're attentive gardeners, we will begin to harvest crops beyond our wildest dreams. I don't know about you, but I want buckets and bushels full of a godly harvest in my life...and garden.

Harvest Time

While rewarding, harvest time can often feel overwhelming, as if everything is coming on at once. Which is why I recommend starting small!

If you have more produce than you can deal with, consider giving some to family, friends, and even your local food bank. During the peak months of harvest in my area, July and August, there is usually always a bag or two of fresh garden produce in the foyer at church for the taking.

Some of the most prolific vegetables are summer squash. Cucumbers and zucchini can easily produce more than you're able to keep up with. In fact, one to two hills (containing three plants each) are more than enough for one family. When harvesting, be sure to lift leaves of cucumbers and zucchini, as often the plants will hide under large leaves. It's best to check your plants daily during the peak of summer production.

Cucumbers are best when harvested small, especially for pickling. Small cucumbers make crunchier pickles. If cucumbers are smooth and turning yellow, they're generally overripe. Small zucchini are favorable for grilling. We slice ours lengthwise, rub them with a little bit of olive oil, sprinkle with salt, and grill for a wonderful side dish.

However, large zucchini can also be hollowed out and stuffed with meat and cheese. They can also be grated for zucchini bread, cake, muffins, pizza crust, and as an addition to sauces. There's not much you can't sneak some grated zucchini into.

* * *

Another favorite zucchini treat is to slice them into thin rounds. Beat an egg, dip zucchini into the beaten egg, drag through seasoned flour or cornmeal, and bake on a cookie sheet at 350 degrees. Flip over at 10 minutes and bake for another 10 minutes. Sprinkle grated cheese on top and let bake for another 2 minutes or until cheese is melted.

We plant our garlic in the fall and harvest in mid-July. There are two kinds of garlic: soft-necked and hard-necked. Hard-necked garlic is ready to harvest when the top four to six leaves turn yellow and wither. Soft-necked garlic is ready to harvest when the stalks fall over.

To harvest garlic, use your hands or a shovel to loosen the bulb. Be careful if using a shovel not to slice into the bulb. Pull up the bulb and knock off the largest of the dirt clods from the roots.

Garlic needs to cure before storing. To cure garlic, let it sit in a warm area with good ventilation for two weeks, more if it's extremely wet or humid. We thread our garlic through a square piece of wire fencing and hang it on our covered back porch. You don't want to let your garlic cure in direct sunlight. The sunlight can burn the garlic and reduce the flavor.

After garlic is cured, trim the roots and brush off the now-dried dirt. Don't remove more than a layer of the garlic's skin as this helps it keep a longer shelf life.

Soft-necked garlic can be braided and hung in your kitchen. Hard-necked garlic can be gathered together by its stalks and stored.

Onions are ready to harvest when their stalks begin to fall over, the same as garlic. Use the same techniques for harvesting. To cure, we put two large screens or wire on a sawhorse and place the onions on top. Let them sit in a dry, well-ventilated area to cure for two to three weeks.

Tomatoes are one of the few fruits that can still ripen on the vine even after the vine is pulled from the soil. If you live in an area with a shorter growing season, you may have tomatoes still on the vine waiting to ripen at the end of the growing season.

If your tomatoes are not under cover and a big rainstorm is moving in or a frost is predicted, pull your tomatoes up, vine and all. Hang the plants in a dry, temperature-protected area where air can circulate. The tomatoes on the vine will continue to ripen over the next week or two, even though they're not in the ground.

If you're harvesting shelled beans (to use as a dried bean) or saving seeds from your beans for next year's planting, use the end of the garden season to do the drying for you. If a rainstorm is moving in before you have time to shell the dried beans on the vine, or before they've fully dried, pull them up, plant and all, just like we do tomatoes. If not fully dried, hang them in a covered dry area. If they are fully dried, but you haven't had time to shell them yet, place them in a large bucket or container and move them to cover until you have time to shell them.

I've had mine in a bucket until close to Christmas before I got around to shelling them out. If there is any moisture on the vines or pod, though, they can start to mold, so you need to be sure they're brittle dry if you're not going to shell them out quickly.

Use the below chart to help you plan your coming harvest.

Plant	My Sow Date	Days to Harvest	My Harvest Date
Beans, pole and bush		60	
Beans, shellies or dry		85+	
Beets		50+	
Broccoli		80+	
Cabbage		70+	
Carrots		55+	
Cauliflower		50+	
Chard		50+	
Corn		60+	
Cucumbers		70+	
Garlic		9 months	
Kale		80+	
Lettuce		50+	
Onions		90+	
Parsnips		120+	

Plant	My Sow Date	Days to Harvest	My Harvest Date
Peas		55+	
Peppers		50+ from planting outdoors	
Potatoes		90+	
Rutabaga		80+	
Spinach		40+	
Squash, summer		50+	
Squash, winter/ pumpkin		90+	
Tomatoes		80+	
Turnips		40+	
Watermelon		70+	

Be sure to also record how many plants you've sown (e.g., two twelve-foot rows, three hills of five plants each, etc.) and your eventual crop yield (e.g., 50 pints canned, 20 cups frozen, etc.). Keeping detailed charts of all this information will be invaluable as you plan next year's harvest!

Preserve

Blessed is the one who perseveres under trial because,
having stood the test, that person will receive the crown
of life that God has promised to those who love him.

JAMES 1:12

*Preserving food is one of my favorite pioneer tasks. There is little
more satisfying than gazing at stores of food you grew and preserved yourself. I have a slight addiction to Mason jars and have
been known to gaze at jars of home-canned goods like one would
a fine piece of art.*

*Even if you can't grow it at home, knowing how to preserve food
when it's in season for use throughout the year is one of the most frugal and rewarding things you can do. While there are certain safety
factors one needs to adhere to with home food preservation, it is an
old-time tradition every home should learn and practice.*

Certain events in our lives forever change us. These moments are preserved in our memories when time crashes around us, never to return to quite the same flow.

My husband and I had been married five years when we decided to try for our first child. Within a month a little stick in a box from the pharmacy confirmed we were expecting our first child. We quickly told our parents, coworkers, and friends, and within a few days it seemed our entire little town knew. Of course, if you've ever lived in a small town, you know how fast news travels.

My first doctor's appointment confirmed I was pregnant, gave us our due date, and provided a list of foods to stay away from during pregnancy. Planning the nursery and browsing the store shelves filled with little bitty garments were our new activities.

I went in for routine bloodwork.

Two days later, the nurse from my doctor's office called me at work. They'd gotten the bloodwork back and needed me to come in first thing the following morning. I gripped the phone. "Why?"

"We suspect an ectopic, a tubal pregnancy. We'll know more when you come in."

Eyes squeezed shut, I drew in a deep breath, refusing to let the tears come. Tears meant it was true. I held onto the hope it wasn't.

The next morning my husband and I sat in the doctor's office. The cold gel from the ultrasound matched the dread settling over me. I searched the monitor for the blinking blip of a heartbeat.

Nothing.

"I'm sorry. The ultrasound confirms the blood test; your pregnancy is ectopic. We need to schedule an emergency surgery tomorrow."

Numbness followed me home. Normally a talkative person, I dreaded picking up the phone and calling my parents and my in-laws with the news. How do you find the words to define a loss you can't begin to understand?

Living over an hour away from the hospital, we had to get up early to get to the surgery. Sitting on the edge of our bed I stared out the window. The gray light of dawn met me. Raindrops streaked the sweaty glass of our bedroom window. *God's crying with us.*

I'd never been in a hospital, and sliding into the hospital gown and bed I felt like I was underwater, pushing against the current. After the nurse put medicine in my IV, I fell asleep. I woke up in the recovery room. My husband sat beside my bed.

The doctor came into the room. "We weren't able to save your fallopian tube. It was too damaged from the fetus."

I stared at him. "Will I be able to have children?"

"It might take you longer, but you should be able to conceive again."

I knew what he wasn't saying. If I had another ectopic pregnancy with my remaining fallopian tube, that would be it. Frustration pushed against my throat. Anger bubbled in my sore stomach.

My husband wasn't allowed to stay with me in the hospital, and I couldn't sleep. I stared at the ceiling most of the night. *Why did you let this happen, God? We did everything right. We were married. You let drug addicts and people who abuse their children have babies, so why not me?*

My husband had to return to work the next day. I longed to go back to work or lose myself in mundane tasks, but recovering from the surgery kept me on the couch or the recliner. Left with only my thoughts and emotions, I spiraled downward.

My phone rang. We still had an old-fashioned phone—the kind with a cord attached. It wouldn't reach to the living room, and I couldn't stand for very long yet. I sat on the cracked linoleum in the kitchen.

One of the pastor's wives from our small town was calling me. We didn't attend their church. But Jesus isn't contained by a denomination or a building. She'd delivered a stillborn baby some years earlier. Tears dripped down my cheeks and plopped onto the linoleum as she shared her heart with me.

She could have chosen to wallow in her pain, to become bitter, or to blame God. Why would a loving God allow these things to happen?

But she'd made a choice to love, to believe God had good things in store for her.

I had the same choice. I could choose to hand all the pain to Him and see how He could redeem it, or I could let it continue to hurt me.

I chose my Redeemer.

In choosing him, I was transformed. The pain brought me back to the cross where He died for me and made me realize what a precious gift that is. God lost a child so I could be free of sin. What greater gift is there? My pain brought me to a place where Jesus reached out His hand and said, "Come walk with me, child."

One night at dinner, years later, my son asked who we most wanted to see when we got to heaven. We took turns going around the table and answering.

When it was my turn I named my Grandmother Revonda, Moses, and my first baby. I explained to my children they had a sibling in heaven who had been in my tummy before them. My face heated and my throat tightened. What would they say?

"You mean I'm not the first?" my son asked.

I shook my head. "You're my firstborn here on earth, but you aren't my first baby."

My four-year-old daughter looked at me. "Are you happy with us?"

Her words squeezed my heart tighter than the tears squeezing my throat. "I'm very happy with you." In that moment I realized how much, more than I could have dreamed ten years ago when I held anger and hurt close.

God brought me full circle. Someday I'll get to be with all my children, but for now I'm resting in Him and what He has for me to do on this earth. His love is bigger than our hurts.

I can honestly say my greatest hurt was what preserved my faith in Jesus.

* * *

I come from a long line of home food preservers. I grew up to the hiss and jiggle of my mother's pressure canner from midsummer through fall. The *ping* of canning lids ensured that we would have food for the winter. It's still one of my favorite sounds. Seriously, I have the urge to fist pump when I hear those pings.

Here on our homestead, we grow as much of our own food as possible and we also preserve as much of that food as we can. Home canning may seem like a lost art, but I'm seeing its resurgence.

I like to can a lot of our food because it's easy to store. Plus, in the event our power goes out, I know all of my canned goods will be just fine. Another reason is because I'm a busy woman and I don't have time to cook a full meal every night. But I can pop open a few jars of my canned food and heat it, and I've got a from-scratch, home-cooked, wholesome meal on the table.

Children are great to show you things you say a lot. Whenever my daughter sees me get out my canning jars and canner she says, "Are we putting this up for winter?"

It makes me smile every time. "Yes, we're putting this up for winter."

* * *

When my husband and I first got married, our favorite box at Christmas was the box from his grandmother. It was filled with her home-canned jars of pickles, popcorn balls, cookies, and strawberry jam.

As I progressed in my canning, I made my own batch of strawberry jam. I knew this was the most coveted by my husband, and the few jars we got from his grandmother didn't last us all year. Knowing we could easily eat two full batches of a jam in a year, I decided to save time and make one large batch with all the berries.

I got out my largest stockpot. Measuring bowls and glops of strawberry juice covered the cramped counters of our kitchen.

I followed the instructions step by step. Eager, I stirred the pot, waiting for the glorious moment when it began to set and jell.

It didn't. I let it simmer longer. And longer.

Maybe it jells after you can it and it cools down, I thought. I ladled my sweet-smelling mixture into my jars, wiped the rims clean, and screwed the rings down over the lids. Onto the rack and submerged into the water bath they went. The processing time ticked by on the clock.

I pulled the gorgeous ruby-filled jars out and set them on a towel to cool. Unable to wait the full 24 hours you're supposed to before touching them (you can disturb the sealing process), I opened one of the jars. Taste test. Perfect. Lick-your-spoon-in-danger-of-eating-the-entire-jar good.

Except one little thing. It was runny. Too runny to spread on warm biscuits, peanut butter sandwiches, or scones. Maybe I hadn't let it cool long enough?

We could use the one jar I'd opened on ice cream or yogurt or swirled into oatmeal. It was still a tasty syrup even if it didn't know it was supposed to be thick jam.

Patience is a virtue I'm working on. I waited the full 24 hours and held another jar up to the light. Did it look thicker? Tipping it, I watched the contents run up the side of the glass.

I'd successfully canned over eight pints of strawberry syrup.

Beyond irritated, I packed the jars off to the pantry shelves. I wasn't going to let them go to waste, but I hadn't planned on syrup. "There must have been something wrong with the recipe or the pectin," I said to my husband.

He shrugged. "Or maybe you did something wrong."

My mouth gaped open. Was he serious? Because it couldn't have been something I'd done...right?

With my jam-making skills in serious humble mode, I asked his grandmother if I could come down for a lesson. She eagerly agreed, and both my mother-in-law and I made two batches of jam with Grandma walking us through it.

Lesson number one in jam-making: You can only make one batch at a time when using regular store-bought pectin. Even though it's the same ratio of ingredients, you cannot double a batch. It won't set.

It's been years now, and I've never had a problem as long as I stick to the small-batch method. My pantry is lined with six kinds of home-made jams and jellies. The only time I have syrup is if I set out to make it.

I've learned not to jump ahead in the kitchen, and God is slowly teaching me the same lesson in my life. Sometimes I wish He'd show me His plan all at once instead of giving me one step at a time. But He knows if He showed me everything at once, I wouldn't be able to take it all in. So in his wisdom, He just shows me the step I need at the time.

Preserving
Choosing Produce

Preserving food at home is one of my favorite pioneer traditions. Even if you're not able to grow everything at home, you can still save considerable amounts of money by putting food up yourself. By purchasing fruits and vegetables when they're in season, you're able to get them at a lower cost than other times of the year. Many times, you can save even more money by purchasing those items in bulk or going to a u-pick farm.

If I don't grow enough of an item myself, I prefer to go to a u-pick farm or farmers' market. A u-pick farm is preferable because you can pick the produce when it's at its prime, not overripe or underripe. Though for jam making, if a portion of your fruit isn't quite at its ripest, it usually has a slightly higher level of natural pectin.

If none of those places are available, become good friends with the produce manager at your local grocery store. They can tell you when the new produce arrives and is freshest.

To take advantage of the low seasonal prices, you'll want to purchase enough of each item to see you through to the following year. This amount will vary for each family.

I don't purchase jam or jelly from the store—ever—so I know I need to make enough to last us until the next berry season. We grow our own raspberries, blueberries, blackberries, and strawberries. However, our strawberry plants don't provide us with enough berries for all the jam we can eat. We're lucky enough to have a u-pick farm a few miles up the road from us. I usually pick their organic strawberries twice during the season. We go through approximately two jars of jam a month, so I like to have two dozen jars (a mixture of different kinds) for the year, with extras to give out as Christmas gifts.

It's a good idea to keep track of what your family eats and goes through in a month and then average that out for the year. Here is a chart of the best times of the year to buy seasonal produce on average. Times for locally grown produce vary slightly by region.

Season	Fruits	Vegetables
January – February	Citrus fruits (oranges, lemons, grapefruit, tangerines), papaya	Broccoli, brussels sprouts, cabbage, cauliflower, kale, parsnips, turnips, potatoes
March – April	Mango, pineapple, rhubarb	Artichoke, asparagus, new potatoes, radishes, spring peas, snow peas
May – June	Apricots, rhubarb, strawberries	Lettuce, new potatoes, spring onion, swiss chard, zucchini
July – August	Blackberries, blueberries, boysenberries, cherries, melons, peaches, plums, raspberries	Corn, cucumbers, eggplant, garlic, green beans, lettuce, okra, onions, peppers (sweet and hot), summer squash, tomatillos, tomatoes
September – October	Apples, dates, figs, grapes, pears, pomegranates	Acorn squash, butternut squash, carrots, garlic, kale, onions, potatoes, pumpkin, spaghetti squash, spinach, winter squash, tomatoes
November – December	Apples, cranberries, dates, pears	Beets, brussels sprouts, cauliflower, carrots, celery, leeks, parsnips, potatoes, pumpkin, rutabaga, sweet potato, swiss chard, turnips, winter squash

Once you purchase your produce you've got several options for preserving it. Of course, we like to eat some of it fresh, but the rest we preserve for year-round eating. The main methods of preserving fruits and vegetables are freezing, dehydrating, canning, fermenting, and root cellar or cold storage techniques. Some herbs can also be preserved in alcohol to make your own tinctures and extracts.

When choosing which method of preserving you'll use, you need to consider how you want to later use the food. For example, if you prefer to use zucchini in stir-fry or in quick breads, then freezing is probably your best option. For quick breads, I grate up my zucchini, squeeze out the excess moisture, and vacuum seal it in two-cup portions. For stir-fry or to add to stews and soups, I either slice it in rounds or dice it before freezing.

I usually use a couple of methods for each food depending upon how I'll be cooking or eating it later.

Freezing

Let's first talk freezing, as this is the method most people have had some experience with. You'll need a freezer and freezer containers, usually freezer bags. I've found our vacuum sealer allows me to get more food into our freezer and does a better job at keeping freezer burn away from the food, prolonging its shelf life. I can also use the vacuum sealer with my dehydrated items. If you plan on preserving or putting up a lot of your own food, you may wish to get one.

* * *

If you don't have a vacuum sealer, freezer bags also work, but for long-term freezer storage, we've found a vacuum sealer has been invaluable.

Berries lend themselves well to being frozen. Some people recommend flash-freezing them before storage—that is, laying them out in a single layer on a tray to freeze them before putting them in a bag. I don't bother with this. I pour raspberries, blueberries, and blackberries straight from my colander into my freezer bag and pop them in the freezer. They rarely stick together, and if they do, I can pull them apart quite easily with my fingers. The key to this is making sure they're not wet before freezing.

Because I use organic methods at home and only purchase or pick organic berries, I don't soak or wash them before freezing. Unless, of course I happen to spill the whole bucket in the field! But I sample berries as I go. Nothing is as good as a sweet, ripe blueberry straight from the bush. I don't go in the house and wash it before I eat it. I don't see the need to do the same before I freeze them either. The one caveat to this is berries grown on the ground, like strawberries. They are low enough to the fertilizer used that there could be cross-contamination. Rinse them well, allow to dry fully, and then freeze. If you're unsure of the growing method, always rinse the berries

You can also freeze berries you plan on making jam or jelly out of later. Usually when the berries are ripe, summer temperatures make you want to do anything other than heat up your kitchen with canning. Toss your berries into the freezer for a cooler day. Plus, frozen and then thawed berries give up their juice more easily, speeding up the cooking process. I also freeze my lemons and limes whole for this same reason when I need them for juicing and as my pectin source.

Some vegetables need to be blanched before freezing. Blanching is immersing the vegetable in either steam or boiling water for a short period of time and then immediately placing the hot food into cold water to stop the cooking process. The reason for this is to stop the enzymes from breaking down the food (causing decay), which will still happen even when frozen.

I tend to be a person who learns from mistakes instead of just following instructions. Something I'm working on. One year I decided to freeze some of our butternut squash and skipped the blanching step, thinking it was unnecessary. I peeled and cubed it and stuck it in the freezer. No matter how I prepared that frozen squash, it never tasted right. It didn't matter how long I cooked it, either—the texture was always a bit hard and woody. I ended up throwing most of it out.

The following year I took the time to prepare it correctly and it worked beautifully. It baked up exactly how fresh squash would, with perhaps a bit less cooking time. Lesson learned.

Below is a list of foods that can be blanched as well as cooking times. Always wash and trim the vegetable before blanching as you would before cooking it. For example, remove ends of beans, trim broccoli and cauliflower to bite-sized pieces, peel and remove seeds from winter squash, and peel root vegetables.

Blanching Times for Freezing Vegetables

- Asparagus: Blanch in boiling water 2 minutes for small stalks, 3 minutes for medium stalks, and 4 minutes for large stalks.

- Beans, green: Blanch in boiling water 3 minutes.

- Beans, lima: Blanch in boiling water 2 minutes for small beans and 4 minutes for large beans.

- Beets: Blanch until tender, then peel and chop to desired size. Blanch in boiling water 25-30 minutes for small pieces and 45-50 minutes for large pieces.

- Broccoli: Most folks prefer steam-blanching rather than boiling. Steam for 5 minutes.

- Brussels sprouts: Blanch in boiling water 3 minutes for small sprouts and 5 minutes for large sprouts.

- Carrots: Blanch in boiling water 3 minutes for slices and 5 minutes for whole carrots.

- Cauliflower: Blanch in boiling water 3 minutes.

- Corn on the cob: Don't use overripe corn. Corn is at its peak and best for eating and preserving when it still has liquid inside the kernel. When pierced, the liquid should look milky. Blanch in boiling water 7 minutes for small ears, 9 minutes for medium ears, and 11 minutes for large ears.

- Corn kernels: With the kernels still on the cob, blanch in boiling water 4 minutes. Allow to cool. Cut kernels off the cob and freeze.

- Greens: Blanch in boiling water 2 minutes. After the ice-water bath, squeeze out excess moisture before freezing.

- Peas: Blanch in boiling water 1½ minutes.

- Rutabagas and turnips: Blanch in boiling water 2 minutes.

- Summer squash: Blanch in boiling water 3 minutes.

- Winter squash: Steam blanch 20 minutes. I prefer to dice my butternut squash into ½-inch cubes. Acorn squash is usually mashed or puréed after blanching and then frozen.

When freezing any food, I find it works best if it's frozen in uniform pieces. All chopped up to roughly the same size. No need to bring out a measuring stick; just eyeball it. This way, when I'm thawing the food, it all thaws out evenly. Be sure to label your frozen food with the date and the portions. Practicing rotation in your pantry and freezer is key to using what you have and not having to throw out old food.

Dehydration

Dehydrating is another form of food preservation. Having an actual dehydrator will open up the kinds of foods you can dehydrate, including making your own powders from milk, eggs, and broth to name a few. However, you can use your oven and the sun to dehydrate some foods.

Dehydration is simply pulling out the moisture from the food. Many people like dehydration for fruits, vegetables, and nuts because if done at a low temperature, the food still retains nearly all of its vitamins and nutrients and is still considered raw.

The most frequently used food in dehydration in most homes is herbs. Those bottles of dried herbs you purchase at the grocery can be made easily at home and for a fraction of the price. I don't know about your grocery store, but some of those tiny bottles run upwards of six or seven dollars apiece.

* * *

Growing your own herbs is easy and something anyone can do. Southern-facing windows are excellent spots for a small herb garden indoors, and most herbs do quite well in containers on the porch or deck. Basil, rosemary, sage, and mint grow very well in containers. Mint and oregano will spread everywhere if not planted in a container to control them.

It's best to pick your herbs in the morning; this is when they have the highest concentration of oil in the leaves, which is where you get the flavor. Bring them indoors and rinse them if they're dusty. Spread them out on a clean, absorbent towel.

If you're using a dehydrator, lay them evenly on the trays. Remember, they'll shrink up considerably, so if you have the liquid liners for your dehydrator, use them to avoid letting the herbs slip through the cracks of the trays.

Don't have a dehydrator? Herbs are simple to dry without the aid of any appliances. When you pick them, leave them on the stem. Break the stem off at the base of the plant. Tie no more than five stems together (the air needs to be able to flow around and through them) and hang them upside-down in a warm area.

You don't want to hang them in direct sunlight. The sun can burn the leaves as they're drying. I use the rafters of the roof on our covered porch; some folks use the kitchen. I've also hung them near the chimney of our woodstove in the early spring when the sun was nowhere to be found and the outside air was a damp mess.

Check them every day or so. If you see any signs of mold or mildew on the leaves, discard them and move the herbs to a drier location.

Depending upon the moisture content in the air, they're usually fully dry within a week. The leaves should be brittle and crumble when you rub them between your fingers. Place your dry herbs in a clean, dry glass jar. I use my smaller Mason jars or old spice jars. You can also find small glass jars with lids in stores or online. When not in use, store your herbs in a cool, dark cupboard.

Although you can simply use a knife to slice or chop all your foods for dehydrating, I've found a mandoline and combination apple peeler and corer make the job go much more quickly.

One of our favorite treats is dried apple slices. I put them through our peeler and corer, which also slices them into even ribbons at the same time. Some fruits, especially apples and pears, will turn brown once exposed to the air. You can avoid this by putting them in a lemon juice bath or dipping them in honey. Honey-dipped apple slices are great dehydrated, but our favorite (and quickest) is cinnamon apples.

Cinnamon Apples

Place a quarter cup of Ceylon cinnamon (or add few shakes of nutmeg or ginger for a slightly different flavor) in either a container with a lid or a large plastic bag. Seal the container and shake until the apple slices are evenly coated. You may add a pinch or two of sugar if your apples are tart. I prefer Honeycrisp, Gala, or Fuji apples, which are usually quite sweet on their own.

Arrange evenly on your dehydrator trays so the apples aren't touching. It's important for the air to circulate freely around the fruit for even drying. Set your dehydrator to its fruit setting or 135 degrees. Check your fruit after a few hours. Drying time will vary depending upon how thick your fruit slices are. I rotate my trays once or twice through the drying process. You can't really dehydrate it too long. The honey slices will remain slightly tacky. When the cinnamon slices are dry, transfer them to a clean, dry glass jar. I store mine in a quart-sized Mason jar in the cupboard for several months.

----

9 Ways to Preserve Apples at Home

1. **Apple Pie Filling.** Is there anything better than lovely jars of home-canned apple pie filling? Yes, there is—diving headfirst into said jar with a spoon. Ever notice how apple prices go up during the holidays? You may can apple pie filling or you may also freeze it. I peel, core, and slice up my apples, add my sugar and spices to the apples, place in either a freezer bag or quart-sized Mason jar, and freeze.

2. **Applesauce.** See instructions on page 75.

3. **Dehydrated Apples.** See instructions on page 69.

4. **Apple Scrap Cider Vinegar.** Yep, make your own lovely fermented apple scrap cider vinegar. You won't believe how easy it is. Place cores and peelings in a clean Mason jar until approximately two-thirds full. Pour water over top until apple scraps are completely submerged. Cover the jar with a breathable towel or cheesecloth and secure with a band. Allow to sit for two weeks, stirring once a day or so. Strain out apple scraps and pour liquid back in a clean Mason jar. Allow to sit and ferment for another 2 to 4 weeks until it takes on a tangy vinegar smell.

5. **Apple Pectin.** You can make your own apple pectin by boiling apples (with cores and peels) until they've turned mushy. Drain the cooked apples through cheesecloth. Cook down the strained liquid until it's slightly thick, then freeze and use as pectin in all your homemade jams and jellies. Slightly underripe apples have higher pectin levels.

6. **Apple Butter.** Fruit butters are a delight and very easy to make.

7. **Apple Jelly.** I love apple jelly because all it takes is apple juice and sugar or honey. That's it, just two ingredients to make a delightful jelly for smearing on pancakes, biscuits, waffles, toast, or by the spoonful.

8. **Fruit Leather.** See instructions below.

9. **Root cellar or cold storage.** Apples hold up well in a cool environment and in proper conditions will store clear through the winter. They prefer temperatures between 30 and 35 degrees with high humidity. However, don't let them freeze or the cell walls rupture and your apple, once thawed, won't be so yummy.

Fruit Leather

You can also make your own fruit leather at home. The easiest fruit leather to make is apple. You'll first make applesauce (see recipe on page 75), which is another staple on our homestead. For making fruit leather, allow the applesauce to cool until warm so you don't burn yourself. I purchased silicone matts for my dehydrator for making fruit leather or drying sticky foods. Pour the applesauce onto the trays, spreading it out to an even thickness. Turn dehydrator to 135 degrees and dry until it resembles leather. Store in a glass jar or airtight container. While warm, you can roll it up or just cut it into strips.

Pears also make a wonderful sauce and leather, so if you have an abundant pear crop or access to pears, use them the same way.

Canning

If you've never canned anything before, I'd encourage you to start out with water-bath canning. Remember the jars of homemade jams and jellies your grandmother made? Those can be safely preserved in a hot pot of boiling water.

Water-bath canning is processing your canned foods in boiling water for a specified amount of time. Acidic foods can safely be canned via the water-bath method. These are jellies, jams, preserves, marmalade, fruits, fruit spread, fruit sauces, tomatoes (with acid added via lemon juice or vinegar), pickles, relishes, and chutneys. All you do is follow a tested recipe, immerse your filled jars in a bath of hot water with a canning rack, and boil them for the set amount of time.

Pressure canning heats your canned food under steam pressure, allowing for much higher temperatures and faster cooking times. All low-acid foods must be canned using a pressure canner. Low-acid foods include vegetables, meat, poultry, and seafood.

I know people used to water-bath can tomatoes without added acid and have not experienced problems. But newer strains of tomatoes have lower acid levels, and unless you can check the pH at home, I wouldn't risk it. Growing and preserving your food is rewarding but hard work. I'd rather know it's done safely and correctly using these guidelines.

***

One of the benefits to pressure canning is you can raw-pack almost all your vegetables and fruits. It will cook fully while it's being canned.

Wash your jars, lids, and bands in hot soapy water and rinse well. You can keep your jars heated in hot water in your canner, but I keep mine in the hot wash water until I'm ready to fill them. Do not boil your lids; keep them in a small saucepan with water on medium-low heat on the stovetop. (If water-bath canning for less than ten minutes processing, sterilize jars by boiling them for ten minutes beforehand.)

* * *

Pint-sized jars hold two cups and quart jars hold four cups. Make sure your pressure canner holds both sizes so you only have to make one purchase.

Fill your jars with prepared recipe. If using the raw-pack method (not precooking or heating the item to be canned), pack the fruit and vegetables into the jar and pour boiling water or syrup over top. Don't fill up to the top; leave space between the food and the top of the jar (refer to chart below for amount of space). I prefer to use the raw-pack method for vegetables as it saves me time. Vegetables are fully cooked when pressure canned so I see no reason to heat my kitchen up any more than necessary, plus, I find I end up with crisper, less mushy vegetables using the raw pack method.

Type of Food	Amount of Headspace to Leave in Jar
Fruit juices, pickles, jams, jellies	¼ inch
Fruits and tomatoes	½ inch
Vegetables, meat, poultry, seafood	1 inch

Remove air bubbles by sliding a knife between the side of the jar and your food. Run it around the outside of the jar.

Wipe the rim and threads of the jar with a damp, clean cloth. Place lids on jars and screw band down until resistance is met. Don't overtighten, but make sure they're fingertip tight.

When dealing with hot jars of food, I've found a jar lifter to be an invaluable kitchen tool. Oven mitts work in a pinch, but if they get wet, you can burn a finger quickly. A jar lifter saves my skin and is well worth the small price it costs.

Place the jars in the canner, making sure the rack is in place. This keeps the jars from sitting directly on the heat source or the bottom of the pot. If the jars aren't on the rack, they can become too hot and burst or crack. If you don't have a rack, you can set the jars on old canning bands or even a folded up towel, just so long as the jars are lifted up and the hot water can circulate beneath and around them. For water-bath canning, make sure the water covers the top of your jars by at least 1 inch of water. Follow the amount of water your manual suggests for your pressure canner. Mine calls for a quart and a half.

Start the time for your recipe when the water is at a full boil for water-bath canning or when the pressure control starts to jiggle. For pressure canning, you'll need to lock your lid into place, but don't put the pressure control on yet. Allow steam to come through the vent for ten minutes. This allows the pressure to build and ensures all of the air has been exhausted from both the canner and the jars of food. If air pockets are left, they can cause uneven heating during canning.

Select the correct pounds of pressure for your food and put your controller in place. Once it begins to jiggle and hiss, at least three to four times per minute, start your timer.

When time is up, allow canner to cool according to the manufac-turer's guide. When canning, this means allowing the canner to cool to air temperature on the stove over time. Never run a hot pressure canner under cool water to cool it down quickly when canning.

Carefully remove the jars with either a jar lifter or an oven mitt. Set the warm jars on a double-folded towel. Allow to cool for 24 hours without moving.

After the jars are cool, test the lids for a seal. Press the center of the lid with your finger. If it doesn't flex, the jar is sealed. Remove the band and store in a cool, dry, dark place like a pantry shelf. If it does flex, you may try and reseal it with another round in the canner, place it in the fridge to eat, or store it in the freezer.

These are some of my family's favorite canning recipes. You can find dozens more for whatever type of food you'd like to preserve, but make sure you're looking at a reputable source that follows up-to-date can-ning and food safety guidelines.

Applesauce

Makes about 4 quarts. My favorite apples for applesauce are Gravensteins. Its twisted, gnarled branches reach out, and when laden with their green and blush of pink, it reminds me of how the garden of Eden must have looked. They're an old-fashioned heirloom apple. My parents have an old Gravenstein tree on their property that produces a bumper crop every few years. On those years, I make up as much applesauce as possible. The flavor is so perfect on its own; I don't add any spices or sugar. If you can get yourself some Gravensteins, grab them up. They're harder to find and we planted one in our orchard last year, but it will take several years before it produces a good-sized crop.

I usually choose seconds (not as high quality) apples for applesauce. While I like a crisp apple for munching on, mealy or softer apples work great for applesauce and prevents them from going to waste, as most people don't like to snack on them.

> **12 pounds of apples**
> **water**
> **1 cup sugar (optional)**
> **¼ cup lemon juice**
> **cinnamon and nutmeg (optional)**

The prep work on your apples will depend upon the equipment you have in your kitchen. **If you have a sieve** (conical shaped with small holes to catch the seeds and skins but allow the cooked food to pass through) or a food mill, then simply put whole apples into a large stockpot one to two layers deep. Add an inch or two of water and cover. With the lid on, bring water to a slow simmer. (Think boiling whole potatoes, but you don't want the water to cover the apples as it would water down the finished sauce too much.) Check your apples at 10 minutes for doneness and water level. You don't want to let the pot boil dry. You can stir the apples around a bit at this point to help prevent the bottom layer from scorching. Apples are done when the skins are split and they're soft all the way through.

Once they're warm, but not hot enough to burn you, run the apples through your sieve or food mill. Put the processed apples back into your stockpot. Use the skins to make homemade vinegar, feed them to the chickens (warning, chickens are very fond of apple scraps), or place them in your compost pile.

If you don't have a sieve or food mill, you'll need to peel, core, and slice your apples. (So go buy one immediately!) Put the apples in a large stockpot about ⅔ of the way full (with enough room to stir) and add a cup of water to prevent sticking. Bring to a boil and allow apples to simmer. Stir frequently to prevent scorching on the bottom. Once soft and cooked through, mash with a potato masher.

Heat the applesauce on medium until it's heated all the way through but not boiling. I generally do not add sugar to my homemade applesauce, but this will depend upon your variety of apples and palate. If I'm using a tart apple or they're a tad underripe, I add the smallest amount of sugar possible. I also like to add cinnamon and a dash of nutmeg. Add lemon juice in and stir. The addition of lemon juice is to ensure the proper level of acidity.

I leave my jars in the hot wash water until right before filling. Rinse jars with hot water and place on a towel folded over in thirds. Pour warm applesauce into jars with a ½ inch headspace. Wipe rim of jar with a clean cloth and place lids and bands on jar.

I put up both pint- and quart-sized jars. The size you choose will depend upon the size of your family and how much you'll eat in one sitting. If I know I'll be doing a lot of baking I open a quart-sized jar. If it's just for snacking, I use the pint-sized jar.

Applesauce is acidic enough it can be safely canned in a water bath. I will often use my pressure canner as it heats up faster and uses less water. In a water-bath canner process pint-sized jars for 15 minutes and quart-sized jars for 20 minutes. In a pressure canner process pint-sized jars at 5 pounds of pressure for 8 minutes and quart-sized jars for 10 minutes.

7 Ways to Preserve Pumpkin

1. **Root cellar or cold storage.** Make sure the pumpkin is mature. The skin should be hard on the outside, and it's best if it's been allowed to mature on the vine. You always want to leave the stem on any squash you harvest to preserve it longer. Pumpkins won't keep in cold storage as long as potatoes or other squashes, but it will be fine for two or three months. Be sure none of the skin of the pumpkin is punctured or blemished for this method. Wash the outside down and make sure it's thoroughly dry and has good air circulation. You can wipe the outside down with vinegar to help get rid of any bacteria that would make it break down faster. Pumpkins like temperatures between 50 and 55 degrees and 50 to 75 percent humidity.

2. **Cook your pumpkin.** There are two ways to cook pumpkin in order to use the following preserving methods. The method I've always used is to cut the pumpkin in half, scoop out the seeds, put it facedown in a roasting pan with about ½ to 1 inch of water, and bake until it's soft. You can also put the whole pumpkin in the oven (provided it's not too big to fit) and roast it. Check it by inserting a knife, similar to a baked potato, and allow the pumpkin to cool before opening it up.

3. **Freeze it.** You can freeze the roast pumpkin in cubes or purée. I usually put cubes of cooked pumpkin in a wide-mouth pint-sized Mason jar because most of my recipes call for 2 cups of pumpkin. It thaws really quickly and I purée it right before using in my recipes. You could put it in plastic freezer bags as well.

4. **Dehydrate it.** You can dehydrate pumpkin in either purée or cubed form.

5. **Pumpkin fruit leather.** Use pumpkin puree, applesauce, and spices and make them into a yummy fall fruit leather (see instructions on page 71).

6. **Pumpkin butter** (NOT a canning option). Pumpkin is low in acid and is only safe when pressure canned, but because pumpkin butter is thick it's not safe to be canned in a pressure canner. Store-bought canned pumpkin items are done with industrial canners that reach much higher temperatures than home models. Homemade pumpkin butter is safe to freeze or store in the fridge.

7. **Canned cubed pumpkin** (the only safe way to can pumpkin). You may can cubes of pumpkin at home, but not pumpkin puree, butter, or pie filling. You put heated pumpkin cubes into the jar, pour heated cooking liquid over the cubes, and process in a pressure canner.

Strawberry Jam

Makes approximately 4 pints.

    8 cups strawberries
    3 cups sugar
    zest from 2 lemons
    ¼ cup lemon juice

Wash jars and bands in hot soapy water. Place canning lids in a saucepan, cover with water, and heat on medium-low heat. Fill water-bath canner with water and put on medium heat.

Mash berries with a potato masher, blender, or immersion blender to desired consistency. I prefer mine chunky, but my husband likes it more pureed.

Place berries, sugar, lemon juice, and lemon zest into large pot. Stir until well combined. Bring berries to a boil. **Grandma's note**: If jam starts to foam, add a pat or two of butter to cut the foam.

Stir frequently to keep sugar from scorching. Simmer on a low boil for 10 minutes.

You can test the set of the jam by the sheeting test. Place a metal spoon in the freezer when you begin making your jam. After the 10 minutes of boiling, use the chilled metal spoon to ladle out a spoonful of jam. Hold the spoon and watch the way the jam drips off of the spoon. If it's little individual drops, jam is not set. If it's big goops, it's almost there. If it comes off the spoon in a sheet or doesn't really drop off at all, then jam is set—yank that baby off the heat! Jam will continue to thicken up, or *set* in canning lingo, as it cools. Jam sets when it reaches 220°. Though the sheeting test works, you'll get a more accurate reading with a thermometer. Use a large pot so your jam heats more evenly. If you have trouble reaching 220°, you may need to add another ¼ to ½ cup of sugar. Be sure to closely monitor your jam so it doesn't scorch! Remove from heat as soon as it reaches the setting temperature.

Place jars on a dish towel. Fill jars, leaving a ¼-inch headspace. A canning funnel will be your best friend during this part. With a clean, damp towel, wipe down rim of jar. Place lids on and screw bands down until finger tight.

Immerse jars in water-bath canner inside the canning rack, making sure water covers the tops of the jars by 1 to 2 inches. Once water is boiling, set timer for 10 minutes and allow jars to process.

When time is up, turn off heat. After 5 minutes, remove jars from canner. Place on a towel folded in thirds in a draft-free area. Allow to cool and set overnight or for at least 12 hours. Check seals. If the center of the lid gives, then store in the fridge and eat soon.

If jars are sealed, wipe down with a damp cloth and store in the pantry out of the light for up to a year.

---

* * *

In the olden days, store-bought pectin was out of the question. I don't think my father's mother ever purchased it. My grandmother shared her knowledge and free pectin source. As you guessed, I'm about to do the same with you.

Pectin is a natural substance found in fruit—usually citrus fruits like lemons and limes. However, green or underripe apples, especially crab apples, also have a good amount of pectin in them. (See page 70.)

Another source of natural pectin can be found in currants. (See recipe for Red Raspberry and Currant Jelly on page 81.)

Old-Fashioned Blackberry Jelly

Blackberry jelly is probably my absolute favorite on fresh, hot-from-the-oven biscuits.

   1 gallon ripe blackberries (16 cups)
   1 large green or slightly underripe apple
   4 to 5 cups sugar

Chop up apple and place it with blackberries in a large pot. With a potato masher, mash up the blackberries. Boil mixture for approximately 15 minutes. Blackberries will release their juices. Put this mixture through a sieve or food mill. You'll end up with about 6 cups of blackberry juice.

If you don't have a sieve or food mill, you can use a jelly bag or cheesecloth to strain the berries. Allow boiled mixture to cool enough to handle and place into the jelly bag or a few layers of cheesecloth. Tie cheesecloth closed and hang over a bowl to collect all of the juice.

Put blackberry juice back into your pot. Stir in sugar until completely dissolved. I always use less sugar to begin with and taste it before adding more. Bring to a boil and simmer for 10 minutes.

Fill clean jelly jars with blackberry jelly, leaving a ¼-inch headspace. Wipe rim clean and place lids and bands on jars. Process in a water bath for 10 minutes.

Red Raspberry and Currant Jelly

Makes four 8-ounce jars.

> **1 cup red currant juice**
> **3 cups red raspberry juice**
> **¼ cup lemon juice**
> **zest of 1 lemon**
> **2 cups sugar**

In a saucepan, stir together the red currant and raspberry juice, lemon juice, zest of lemon, and sugar. Bring to a hard boil and boil for 10 minutes, stirring often to keep mixture from scorching. After 10 minutes, use the drip test to check the set of the jelly.

Depending upon how ripe your berries are, I always recommend doing a taste test, especially with tart berries. Be careful, it's hot—don't burn your tongue. Add more sugar if desired to taste.

If jelly is still too runny, allow to continuing boiling for 4 minutes and check again. The longest I've ever had to let mine boil was 25 minutes. This jelly has always set quite firmly for me.

Once jelly has reached its jelled point, pour into prepared jars, leaving a ¼-inch headspace. Wipe rims clean and place on lids and bands. Set jars into prepared water-bath canner. Bring water to a boil and allow jars to process for 10 minutes. Turn off heat and wait 5 minutes before placing jars on a towel folded in thirds. After 12 to 24 hours check for seal. If any jars haven't sealed, place in fridge to eat now or store them in the freezer. Wipe outside of jars clean and store in a cool, dark place until ready to eat.

If you don't wish to can your jelly, you can also freeze it for freezer jam.

---

* * *

A friend of mine had an overabundance of red currants and invited me to come pick them. They're a fairly tart berry, so we much preferred them in a jelly rather than straight off the bush.

We have a row of red raspberries on our homestead. Interestingly enough, our chickens don't seem to care for the raspberries. They like to lounge beneath their leaves for shade but I've yet to catch one of them snitching a low-hanging ripe berry. But I've still got my eye on them, you can bet.

I paired the raspberries and red currants in a brightly festive jelly. The deep reds from both berries make me want to hang the jars from the branches of the Christmas tree. You did know I love Mason jars, right?

We've been talking sweets, but now we're moving into pickles. Pickling foods as a preservation method stretches back hundreds of years. Typically, most people think of cucumbers when they hear the word *pickles*, but pretty much every vegetable can be pickled.

Our favorite pickled foods are pickled asparagus and garlic. Our family has been known to pick a fight over who gets the last jar if we didn't put up enough. In fact, my siblings ask me for jars of our pickled asparagus as their Christmas gift.

It's important to note that the only way vegetables can be safely canned via the water-bath method is with pickling. This is because the vinegar brings the acidity level up enough to prohibit the growth of botulism. Always use 5% vinegar when canning and never lower the amount of vinegar used in a pickling recipe or change the vinegar ratio to water.

Pickled Garlic

Makes approximately nine 6-ounce jars. It's important to use canning salt in this recipe as it doesn't have any additives that can discolor your food.

> **135 cloves peeled garlic (depending upon the size of
>   the garlic, about 15 per jar)**
> **3 cups vinegar**
> **1½ cups water**
> **2 Tablespoons canning salt**
> **9 teaspoons mustard seed**
> **9 teaspoons black peppercorns**
> **red chili flakes (optional)**

Peel your garlic. Fill your water-bath canner with water and begin heating on medium-high heat on the stove. You want to bring it to just below a boil. Wash your jars and bands in hot soapy water; leave jars in hot wash water until ready to fill with garlic and brine. Pour vinegar, water, and canning salt into a saucepan and bring to a boil. Stir until salt is completely dissolved.

Set jars on a folded towel on the counter. Place 1 teaspoon of mustard seeds and black peppercorns in each jar. Add a pinch of hot pepper flakes if you like a little heat in your food. (Whenever making pickles we do two batches—one with added hot pepper for my husband and one without for me.)

Pack jars with the peeled garlic, leaving a ¾-inch headspace. Don't pack tightly. You want the brine to be able to flow around the heads of garlic. Pour hot brine over the garlic, leaving a ½-inch headspace. If you run short on brine, add vinegar to reach the proper level. Run a knife or spatula around the outer edge of the jar to remove any air bubbles.

Wipe rim of jar with a clean towel. Place canning lids on jar and screw bands down until fingertip tight. Set jars into canning rack and place in hot water bath, making sure at least one to two inches of water covers the top of the jars. Bring water to a full rolling boil.

Start processing time when water reaches a full boil. Process jars for 10 minutes. Turn off heat and remove lid for 5 minutes. Using a jar lifter, place jars on a towel folded in thirds on a stable surface away from any drafts. Leave jars for at least 12 hours. Check for seals. If any jars didn't seal, store in the fridge.

Though we have opened jars of pickled garlic a week or two after making them, it's best to let them set for a month or so to develop their full flavor. Pickled garlic is wonderful to eat all by itself, but also good added to dishes, salads, or spaghetti. The brine is delicious poured over rice, in salad dressings, or in marinades.

For a delicious variation, place peeled garlic on a rimmed baking sheet. Drizzle with olive oil and roast at 350° for 20 minutes. Pack jars as per recipe and enjoy roasted pickled garlic!

Pickled Asparagus

Makes 6 quarts. As with any pickling, fresh vegetables will give you the best pickles and have the most crunch. A simple tip to see if asparagus is fresh is to snap it in half. It should break cleanly without any strings and you should hear a "snap" noise. If the spear is stringy or limp, the asparagus is not fresh.

We can eat a jar in one day just as it is, but pickled asparagus is wonderful when wrapped in a piece of ham or turkey with a filling of cream cheese. Be warned, they're so good you'll need to make more than one batch to last you through the year.

> **180 spears of asparagus (depending upon size, about 30 spears per quart jar)**
> **8½ cups vinegar**
> **4½ cups water**
> **6 Tablespoons pickling salt**
> **1 to 2 cups sugar**
> **1½ teaspoons celery seed**
> **12 teaspoons mustard seed**
> **12 teaspoons dried dill weed (or use 2 heads fresh dill to each jar)**
> **12 cloves peeled garlic**
> **red pepper flakes (optional)**

Place water, vinegar, salt, sugar, and celery seed in a large pot and bring to a boil. Stir until salt and sugar is dissolved. Fill water-bath canner with water and heat water to almost a boil.

Wash jars in hot, soapy water. Wide-mouth jars are easiest to use when packing asparagus. Rinse jars and place 2 teaspoons of mustard seeds and dried dill (or two heads of fresh dill) and 2 cloves of garlic at the bottom of each jar.

Rinse asparagus in cold water. Measure and chop off ends so that the heads of the asparagus come to a ½-inch headspace. Pack tightly. I find it easier to place jars on their sides when packing asparagus.

Once jars are packed, pour hot brine over the asparagus to a ½-inch headspace. Run a knife or spatula around outer edge of jar to remove any air bubbles. Wipe rims clean, set lids on top, and screw bands down to fingertip tight. Place jars in canning rack or basket and place in water bath.

Bring water bath to a rolling boil. Process jars for 10 minutes. Turn off heat and remove lid for 5 minutes. Carefully place hot jars on a towel folded in thirds in a draft-free area. Let sit for at least 12 hours without touching.

Check to make sure jars have sealed. If any have not, store in fridge. Try not to eat asparagus for at least two weeks for the flavor to set, and wait six weeks for the fullest flavor to develop.

Chapter 4

Cook

Go, eat your food with gladness.

ECCLESIASTES 9:7

With today's mainstream society and the convenience of store-bought or processed ready-made food, cooking from scratch is becoming a lost art. Even many cookbooks contain processed foods in the ingredient list, like a can of condensed soup or packet of such-and-such mix.

Our great-grandparents cooked before there were mixes for everything, and the only canned foods they used were those they'd canned themselves. I realize not everyone can grow and can all their own food. However, you can still provide wholesome, from-scratch meals for your family. This chapter will show you how.

We're referring you to a specialist."

Not what you want to hear when you're sitting in your doctor's office. The hairs on the back of my neck stood at attention. "What does that mean?"

"We've done everything we know how and your symptoms still aren't being managed. We think it's time to refer you to someone else." A tiny niggling of fear shivered its way down my spine. A specialist meant my regular doctor thought something was really wrong.

If you've ever suffered from heartburn, you'll understand my plight. I was on the maximum dose of prescription proton pump inhibitors, taking another medication to coat my stomach and act as a chemical Band-Aid three to four times a day. Despite all of this a constant fiery trail burned from my stomach clear up the back of my throat, like I'd swallowed a double shot of raw jalapeno juice. Sleep evaded me night after night.

The night before my appointment I stood in the middle of our dark kitchen, not wanting to turn on the lights and wake anyone. Minutes ticked by, a steady march of the clock toward dawn, but the burning inside my chest refused sleep to come to my exhausted body. I don't like milk unless it's holding hands with chocolate or chai tea. But I slugged back a swallow anyway. If it would bring me enough relief to fall asleep, I'd gag down a bit.

The cold splash of milk chased its way down into my stomach. For a brief moment, blessed relief. It didn't last.

The next day I sat in the specialist's office.

After telling him my story, he glanced over my chart notes. "Normally someone with your symptoms is overweight and inactive, but you're not either of those."

Um, thanks?

"We'll schedule you for an endoscopy and see what's going on.

You've been on the medicine for a couple of years and I'd really like to see you get off it."

Yeah, me too. Especially if we could find something that would work.

The morning of the endoscopy my husband drove me to the appointment. Much as I like jewelry, the little paper hospital brace-let is never becoming.

After the procedure I listened to the doctor explain what they'd found. "There's definitely erosion to both the esophagus and upper part of the stomach. We don't think it's cancerous, but we took a biopsy to be sure. You do have signs of cell change. I'd also really like to see you go off the medicine. We don't like to see people on it for as long as you've been. If you don't get the acid under control, it will continue to erode your skin and put you at a higher risk for cancer."

How could I go off the medicine? I was using the maximum dose and I was barely coping. My face may have screwed up in an unflat-tering fashion.

The doctor handed me a stack of papers. "This is a list of foods to start cutting out."

I skimmed over it. No coffee? No chocolate! I only needed to read the first two items and shoved the papers into my purse.

"Stick to the list and try to start tapering off your meds. I'll call you in a few weeks."

After sitting down and going over the paper, I realized this was time to get serious. God had given me this opportunity to change my health. I could squander it with stubbornness over foods I loved, or I could do what was hard but needed. Did I want to continue down this path, unable to sleep, and have my cells turn into cancer?

First thing I did was cut out all soda pop. I was a hardcore diet soda fan. Like drank one to two a day, every day. At least, until the last six months when I'd open up a pop in the afternoon and within twenty minutes my stomach would ache. I'd cut back considerably, but I still indulged in my ice-cold fizzy beverage a few times a week.

Three o'clock in the afternoon would hit and I craved a pop.

Especially at work, where the Coke machine hummed to me from the side of the room like a mother singing a lullaby. And saying goodbye to coffee left me with a withdrawal headache for a few days. I might have been a tad bit hard to be around. Remember, I'm from the Pacific Northwest, the birthplace of Starbucks. We seriously have a drive-thru coffee stand on every block. Even my tiny little no-stoplight-for-40-miles town has two coffee stands. You know, in case one is full or you down the entire coffee before you've driven two blocks and come upon the next one.

I began to read the ingredient labels on the foods and beverages my family was eating and buying. Do you know how many foods high fructose corn syrup is in? Let me tell you, if you read every label of the food in your pantry and fridge, it's likely to be on almost all of them.

Now, I'm not a nutritionist or a doctor, but after doing some research, this was one item I was adamant about not consuming. In fact, if I don't know how to pronounce an ingredient or don't know what it is, or if it has a number sign and numeral attached to it, I'm not comfortable eating it or feeding it to my family.

I believe the food I eat should have simple ingredients, with as little altering or processing as possible, and it should most definitely begin to mold or break down when left out for a while. Ever wonder why store-bought bread will stay good for weeks on end but homemade bread will mold by the end of the week? That might make a gross but compelling science project for the next science fair.

After eliminating soda pop, coffee, and high fructose corn syrup, I was able to quit one of the stomach medications altogether and began a slow taper off of the other med. It took about three months before I was medication free.

I'd like to tell you it was a breeze, so easy, but giving up soda pop was hard. There were days I craved the beverage like a dancer craves a song. But for the first time in years, I was able to lie down at night without a river of lava scorching my throat. Over the months it did get easier.

It's now been four years and I can tell you I don't crave soda at all. In fact, I'm not sure I could drink one now. Still, I won't put it to the test.

I won't test it because I know how hard a battle I fought to get here. I don't want to undo that work.

So many times we just want the easy fix. We want to take a pill and make it all better. There have been many times in my life where I just wanted God to wave a magic wand and make everything better. I didn't want to go through the battle. I didn't want to wade through the hurt, the ugly, and the hard.

I just wanted the pretty *after* picture.

While God can and sometimes does reach down and perform miracles, most of the time, this isn't the case. For good reason, too. Most times, the easy way only temporarily fixes the problem. We wipe our brow and utter a praise or two, but then we go on our way, reverting back to old habits because we weren't forced to change.

Easy fixes aren't real fixes; they're just delay tactics. And when left too long, those delays can harm us—merely treating a symptom and not the root of the problems. Our Creator knows us. He knows we tend to be lazy and we want to take the easy way out. He also knows that in order for us to change and to lean on Him, He has to let us experience the hardships.

> Consider it pure joy, my brothers and sisters, whenever you face trials of many kinds, because you know that the testing of your faith develops perseverance. Let perseverance finish its work so that you may be mature and complete, not lacking anything (James 1:2-4).

It's not that God is cruel; He just knows us. Knows we don't change or lean on Him when things are easy. We need the steep roads of the mountain, the gut burning, and the scald of tears to reach the end of ourselves and the beginning of Him.

I would have never reached these places or known God as a friend if I'd been given the easy out. If He'd simply solved the problem for me instantly, I wouldn't have grown. If there's one thing I'm certain of in this life, it's that hard times are going to come, and God is going to meet me in them and travel up the mountain road with me.

* * *

Because we don't eat a huge amount of bread in my family anymore, I will bake two loaves of bread, cut them in half, and freeze half-loaves. When we need bread I'll thaw a half loaf at a time to avoid letting any get moldy or go to waste. Plus, I usually only have to bake bread once or twice a month using this method.

Bread products do amazingly well when frozen. I whip up a double batch of biscuits and flash freeze the cut biscuits on a cookie sheet. After about thirty minutes in the freezer, or when I remember them, I place them in a freezer bag. When we want biscuits, I bake them frozen as I would fresh biscuits. They turn out beautifully.

Real Coffee, Real Chocolate

The beginning of my real-food journey began that day in the specialist's office. It started with cutting out soda, coffee, chocolate, and high fructose corn syrup. But it's continued to evolve and shape my life in ways I'd have never imagined.

First off, in case you were crying into your coffee for me, I found a way to still enjoy coffee almost daily. It's called a cold-brew system. You see, the oils in coffee contain most of the acid. Hot water brings these oils out into the coffee. But not so with cold-brewed coffee.

You take coarsely ground coffee grinds and pour cold water over them. Allow the mixture to seep for eight to twelve hours or overnight. Then strain it and store in the fridge for up to two weeks. You can also purchase a cold brewing coffee system with a filter, a container to brew the coffee, and a carafe for the strained coffee.

After the coffee is brewed with cold water, you can either enjoy it cold or add hot water or milk to make it a warm beverage. All I can say is I'm very happy to have found a way to enjoy my coffee without all the acid. And the frugal homesteading part of me adores the no-power-needed aspect.

I've also found I can eat dark chocolate. I do purchase an organic brand now and have found that a few pieces of dark chocolate (at least 70 percent cocoa) satisfies my cravings and doesn't bother my stomach.

These were the first items I cut out or switched, but it's been a journey in our home to finding more natural and healthier products. In fact, the last time I went grocery shopping it dawned on me that I purchase hardly anything from the inner aisles of the store. It's fresh vegetables and fruit, milk, cheese, nuts, and pantry staples such as salt, sugar, honey, and whole grains or seeds like quinoa. A far cry from the days of canned soups and boxes of nearly ready-made meals or desserts.

Before I share any more about this, I want to address something. Don't let your food and eating become a religion. I've seen more heated debates about the kinds of food people eat than I have over politics. Some people only eat organic, some are gluten-free, some are dairy-free, some believe we shouldn't eat animals, and the list goes on and on.

> Therefore let us stop passing judgment on one another. Instead, make up your mind not to put any stumbling block or obstacle in the way of a brother or sister. I am convinced, being fully persuaded in the Lord Jesus, that nothing is unclean in itself. But if anyone regards something as unclean, then for that person it is unclean. If your brother or sister is distressed because of what you eat, you are no longer acting in love. Do not by your eating destroy someone for whom Christ died. Therefore do not let what you know is good be spoken of as evil. For the kingdom of God is not a matter of eating and drinking, but of righteousness, peace and joy in the Holy Spirit (Romans 14:13-17).

I have fallen prey to this myself; don't think I'm exempt. When we're passionate about something, it's very easy to slip into the thought we're right. I've looked at things in lunch boxes and thought, *I'd never let my kids eat that.* I'm not always a pretty person on the inside. Left to myself, I'm judgmental and prideful.

But thankfully, God hasn't left me to myself.

While I do believe in eating healthy and caring for our bodies, it's not my job to reform everyone's kitchen. I can share changes we've made that have had a positive outcome, but I shouldn't condemn someone who doesn't eat or cook the way I do.

Flour

I began researching the flour we purchase from the store. Ever wondered why every package says *enriched with vitamins*?

Bear with me a minute here. Flour is made from a ground-up wheat berry. It's actually a hard kernel, not a squishy berry like a piece of fruit. This wheat berry is composed of three parts. The first part of the wheat berry is the bran, which is the hard outside part. The second part is the germ and holds the wheat oil. The third part is the endosperm, and this is the part regular flour from the store is made from.

Once the germ is exposed to air during the grinding process, it has a short shelf life before the oil turns rancid. Therefore, this part isn't used in store-bought flour, even whole wheat. However, it's where most of the vitamins and nutrients are stored. This is why store-bought flour says *enriched with vitamins*—because they've been taken out.

∗ ∗ ∗

I grind most of our own flour at home now. I do purchase a small amount of organic all-purpose flour because some baked goods just don't have the light texture without it. There are two types of grain mills for home use, a manual or electric grain mill. Both have good features, but what you intend to use them for will determine which is right for you. A manual grain mill doesn't require electricity and can be used with oil products like beans or nuts. An electric mill can grind a large amount of flour at once and can be adjusted with the flip of a switch. Whichever you choose, you'll be delivering your family a fresher, more nutrient-packed flour.

This reminds me of how we try to add things back into our lives when we know a vital, life-sustaining part is missing. We search for the answer online, through advice from friends, in self-help books, in the newest organization tool, in the latest exercise fad, in a new diet, in a different way of ordering our day. We push and stuff different things into our schedule and routine, hoping it will be the missing thing.

For a little while, it may seem like we've found the answer. Like when you're in the honeymoon phase with a new boyfriend or girlfriend. Everything about them makes you smile, you can't wait to hear them laugh, and they consume your every thought.

While some of these things may work for a short time, or even a long time, eventually we realize something is missing. It gnaws at our insides. The vital, life-giving thing we're searching for is right there, but we pass it by. It's Jesus.

He is our substance, our daily bread. Without Him we are nothing.

Have you ever noticed all of the references to food in the Bible? Jesus is the bread of life. Salt and yeast are mentioned in many verses. When you cook from scratch and understand how ingredients work, it helps us understand these verses even more.

Salt

Salt is a funny thing. We need a small amount to heighten the flavor of whatever it is paired with. A bit of salt actually brings out the sweetness of desserts. Anyone else love salted caramel? Our food would be quite bland without salt.

One year I decided not to use salt when I canned our green beans. I really have no idea why I came upon this decision. It might have been some crazy notion to keep costs down, but I've since learned some things are worth the price.

The first jar I opened was so bland we couldn't eat it without adding salt. Normally, our home-canned green beans are the one vegetable my kids ask for and I have no trouble getting them to finish. My son said, "Mom, what's wrong with these?"

Since I'd canned them during the summer and we didn't start in on the current year's harvest until fall, I'd half forgotten about not adding the salt. "Nothing's wrong with them. Just eat your vegetables."

After filling all the water glasses and finally sitting down to eat my dinner, I forked up a large bite. My nose screwed up. "What's wrong with these beans?"

Then I remembered. No salt. I grabbed the saltshaker and passed it around. Even with the addition of salt, they still didn't taste the same as the jars with salt added at the time of processing. I learned an important lesson: Don't try and leave out the salt altogether.

> You are the salt of the earth. But if the salt loses its saltiness, how can it be made salty again? It is no longer good for anything, except to be thrown out and trampled underfoot (Matthew 5:13).

If salt loses its saltiness, our taste buds suffer. If we lose the saltiness in our faith, we suffer.

Yeast

When I first began baking my own breads, I patiently waited for the dough to double in size. I nestled the dough in the mixing bowl, covered it with a tea towel, and set the timer so I'd be sure and remember to punch it down.

An hour went by and I lifted the corner of the towel. Um, wasn't the dough supposed to be almost to the rim of the bowl? Was my timer broken? (I have a natural inclination to assume it's never me but something else.)

Perhaps the dough wasn't warm enough. My woodstove ticked with heat. I plopped the stainless steel bowl on top of the stove, right next to the chimney. *That ought to heat it up.*

Another hour went by and I checked the dough. Still no rise. I dumped the dough out onto the counter to form it into two loaves. The bottom of the dough had a slight crust on it. Apparently I'd cooked the dough.

Fine, we'd eat unleavened bread because this stubborn—er, frugal—baker wasn't about to let all those ingredients go to waste. Still, a bit of time went by before I tried baking my own bread at home again.

Great bakers aren't born, they're taught. While some people do seem to have a natural knack in the kitchen, everyone learns by trial and error.

Thankfully, there are a lot of folks willing to lend their experience to the rest of us. So here's the thing with yeast: If the water's too hot you'll kill it, if the water's too cold it won't activate. Lukewarm water is best for activating your yeast. If your home is cool, you'll want to avoid using a metal bowl. Metal bowls cool quickly and don't retain heat as well as wooden or glass bowls.

The top of the refrigerator is often a warm place to let the dough rise, or you can turn on the oven light (not the oven) to create a warm incubator for your dough. And trust me on this: During the rising time, keep your dough off the top of the woodstove when it's burning!

Most recipes require two and a quarter teaspoons of yeast for the entire recipe. Worked through the batch of dough, it does its job, making the rest of the ingredients rise, which creates air pockets and the chewy lightness we desire in our breads.

> He told them still another parable: "The kingdom of heaven is like yeast that a woman took and mixed into about sixty pounds of flour until it worked all through the dough" (Matthew 13:33).

A small amount of yeast can transform a large amount of flour—just like a small amount of faith can transform our lives. Each decision we make to follow God and His Word is like working another grain of yeast into the flour of our lives.

I hope you begin making more of your own food at home from scratch, and I hope the next time you measure out salt and yeast, you remember these verses. What a reminder Jesus gave us right there in the cupboard of our kitchens about how we're to live for Him. He wants to be a part of our everyday life. May we think of Him every time we start playing with flour in the kitchen.

Then Jesus declared, "I am the bread of life. Whoever comes to me will never go hungry, and whoever believes in me will never be thirsty" (John 6:35).

* * *

As I began paying close attention to ingredient labels, I found that in order to stay away from items that triggered my reflux or I believe to be harmful to our health, I had to make the food myself.

Because we already live rurally and practice self-sufficiency, we had a decently stocked pantry and food storage. Cooking from scratch was a matter of changing out a few staples to better options and stocking more basic ingredients I could then turn into a variety of recipes.

Have you ever noticed when you run to the store for one particular item you usually end up grabbing a few more items than you intended? I've found by keeping a good stock of staple items I can make many different dishes from basic ingredients. This has significantly lowered our food bill. I'm not limited on making a meal because I don't have a certain mix or can of something to make the recipe.

Here is my basic list for having on hand in your food pantry. You can choose which items you stock from the list and you don't have to stock each item, but you will need at least one from each category.

Acids
- apple cider vinegar
- concentrated lemon juice
- lime juice
- whole lemons
- whole limes

* * *

I purchase whole lemons and limes when they're on sale and freeze them whole for use throughout the year.

Fats
- organic cold-pressed coconut oil
- extra-virgin olive oil
- avocado oil
- butter and/or lard

Flour
- whole wheat pastry
- organic all-purpose
- spelt
- hard white wheat berries
- soft white wheat berries
- gluten-free flour (coconut, almond, oat, buckwheat)

Grains
- quinoa
- organic cornmeal
- rice
- oatmeal (not instant)

Sweeteners
- organic sugar
- evaporated cane juice
- honey
- maple syrup
- molasses
- rapadura
- stevia

Beans
- black beans
- pinto
- white
- kidney
- garbanzo

Salt
- sea salt
- canning salt
- curing salt for meat curing projects

Dairy
- milk
- cheese
- buttermilk
- yogurt
- kefir

Nuts
Unsalted raw nuts are best as you can roast them, make your own candied nuts, make your own nut butters, toast them for texture in soups or on casseroles, add them as toppings for muffins, cakes, and breads, or eat them plain.

***

Using bone-in cuts or whole poultry will allow you to then make your own stock and broth after you've used the meat. What we don't raise ourselves, I purchase either organically or grass-fed. At the very least, I look for no-hormone or no-antibiotic labels.

Meat
- beef
- pork
- poultry
- fish
- lamb

Spices
- cayenne pepper
- celery salt
- Ceylon cinnamon
- chili powder
- cloves (whole and ground)
- cumin
- curry
- ginger
- mustard (whole and ground)
- nutmeg
- red pepper flakes
- pepper
- paprika
- onion powder
- garlic powder
- turmeric

Herbs
- basil
- dill
- oregano
- parsley
- rosemary
- sage
- thyme

Chocolate
I stock both powdered cocoa and organic chocolate chips

Leavening items
- baking soda
- baking powder
- cream of tartar
- active dry yeast (store yeast in the fridge for best results)

* * *

Lard can be used just as you would butter or coconut oil. I use lard in place of any recipe calling for shortening. Lard rendered at home is a good choice as it's not hydrogenated and doesn't contain dairy for those with sensitivities. Shortening is highly processed and contains GMO products.

When rendering lard, I highly recommend only using fat from organic and pasture-raised pigs. Since we raise our own, I know exactly what's going into my lard. But my favorite reason for using lard is the flavor. It makes delightful pie crusts and pastry items.

I believe using things grown on our land or close to where we live is better not only for ourselves but those in our community, and ultimately the country and world. Growing coconuts where I live or olives to make my own oil is not a possibility. While I do use coconut and olive oil, it has to be shipped a long way to get to me. Many resources must be used to make the packaging, house the equipment to press the oil, and fuel to ship it. I don't personally know the people or even the land it's being farmed from.

When we don't have pigs, I can get lard from our local butcher or another pig farmer. I believe supporting those close to home is important. I also receive joy in using a part of the animal that would otherwise be thrown out and wasted.

Baking with lard is pretty much the same as using coconut oil or butter, except it does tend to melt a tad faster. I add a bit more flour when using it in biscuits and pie crusts.

There are two types of lard. The lard around the kidneys and organs of the animal is referred to as leaf lard. This is considered the purest form and best for baking. The other lard is the back fat of the animal and is good for general cooking.

To get started, freeze the lard. It's easiest to work with if you freeze it first. Allow it to partially thaw for about two hours on the kitchen counter.

Chop it up in 1- to 2-inch cubes. You need the pieces of fat to be uniform to avoid scorching and uneven cooking. You want it small to release the oils. Some people will ask the butcher to grind the fat up first for easier rendering. Note: While chopping the lard, your knife and cutting board will become slick. Use caution!

Put ¼ cup of water in the bottom of your slow cooker. As the fat is starting to melt, you don't want it to scorch on the bottom. The water will cook off during the rendering. Fill your slow cooker with lard to the very top and cook on high for 45 minutes to 1 hour. Once it starts to melt, turn down the slow cooker to low. My slow cooker tends to cook on the hot side, so I turned down mine to low and left the lid off for most of the rendering process.

Stir the lard every 20 minutes or so. After the liquid has reached the top of the lard, you're ready for the first rendering. Depending upon the amount of lard you're rendering, the time it takes for this to happen will vary. I did four and a half quarts at once and it took almost three hours for the first rendering. Place a strainer or sieve lined with a layer of cheesecloth over a large bowl. Pour the rendered lard through. Put the contents of the strainer/ sieve back in the slow cooker and continue cooking.

Allow the rendered lard to cool for approximately ten minutes. After lard has cooled, pour into wide-mouth Mason jars. If you don't wait for the lard to cool a bit, you run the risk of cracking your jars. Let lard continue to cool to room temperature before putting on lids and placing in the fridge. Be sure to wipe down the outside of the jars to remove any grease residue.

Mark the first rendering. I simply use a permanent maker and put a 1 on the lid for the first rendering and so on for the next two. Your first rendering is the most pure. It will have virtually no pork flavoring and is perfect for baking pastries, cookies, and cakes. The second rendering will be slightly darker in color and is still fine for biscuits, pie crusts, corn bread, and more savory dishes. The third rendering will be the darkest, has the most pork flavor, and is best used as a cooking oil for frying. All the renderings will be yellow in their liquid form, but will turn white as they cool. Once solid, the first rendering will be snow white.

Store your lard in the fridge. Lard should be fine on the shelf, but I prefer to store mine in the fridge to avoid any of that work turning rancid. It's good in the fridge for six months. The jars I'm not using go in the freezer where they'll stay good for at least a year.

Truthfully, I've found it much more frugal to make dishes myself from scratch. The food tastes better, and when you count the time it takes to drive to the store, park the car, take kids to the bathroom, go through the aisles, wait in line at the checkout, get kids and groceries into the car, start to pull out from the parking lot only to have kids say they have to go potty again, it's faster to make it at home as well.

After numerous power outages in our area of the country—and after a mudslide took out the main highway for almost three weeks—I've also learned the benefit of having a food supply at home. Not only does it help when the store isn't open or we can't get to it, but it also saves me time by allowing me to shop from our pantry instead of the store shelves.

I can make a few cups of sauce to replace those cans of condensed soups in three minutes for about fifty cents, and that's using organic ingredients.

Homemade White Sauce/Gravy or Condensed Cream of Soup Replacement

Here's my recipe for replacing condensed cream soups in your dishes. It also makes a really good white sauce for pizza.

> **3 Tablespoons butter (coconut oil if you're dairy-free)**
> **3 to 4 Tablespoons flour (organic cornstarch or**
>   **arrowroot powder for gluten-free)**
> **1 cup milk (for a richer sauce, use cream; for a**
>   **dairy-free option, use chicken broth)**
> **¼ teaspoon salt**
> **dash of pepper**

In a saucepan, melt butter (or fat of choice) over medium-low heat. Whisk in flour. It will make a thick paste. Slowly whisk in your liquid. Bring to a simmer (barely a boil), adding more liquid if it becomes too thick. It will thicken up a bit on cooling. Remove from heat and stir in salt and pepper.

You can add in sautéed mushrooms for a cream of mushroom flavor. Sauté minced garlic and onion for another flavor add-in, depending upon your dish.

If it's too thick, add more liquid; too thin, add in a little bit more flour (or thickener of choice) and allow it to simmer for another minute or so. Be sure to stir frequently to avoid scorching the bottom of the sauce. The longer it cooks, the thicker it will become.

Honey Whole Wheat Buttermilk Sandwich Bread Recipe

Homemade bread is another item I replaced at home. After going through all the ingredient labels at the store I was appalled at the long list of things in our bread, high fructose corn syrup and loads of sugar being just some of many.

I'm going to let you in on a little secret. Buttermilk. Yes, buttermilk is a cultured food that makes many folks turn up their nose. I mean, have you tasted it? It's sour. (My father loves the taste of straight buttermilk, so for those of you who do, he's right there with you.) But it does delightful things to baked goods. Buttermilk makes your baked goods lighter, and the texture—oh, the texture. You'll have to try it to believe it, but buttermilk is my go-to.

This is my favorite honey whole wheat buttermilk bread recipe. It makes scrumptious sandwiches and worth-getting-out-of-bed-early French toast.

4½ teaspoons yeast
1¼ cups warm water
¼ cup honey
6 Tablespoons melted butter
2 cups buttermilk
1 egg (optional)
8 cups freshly ground hard white wheat (or use 9½
    cups all-purpose flour)

**a scant ¼ cup vital wheat gluten (Omit if using
all-purpose or bread flour. Vital wheat gluten gives
whole wheat flour a better rise, but it's optional.)
1 Tablespoon sea salt**

Add yeast, warm water, and honey to a mixing bowl and mix. Let proof for about 5 minutes. (Proofing means water turns frothy and yeast is active.) Add in the rest of the ingredients until dough starts to pull away from the side of the bowl. Knead with dough hook for 4 minutes if using a stand mixer. If kneading by hand, knead for 6 minutes.

Let rest for 10 to 15 minutes. Lightly coat counter with oil to keep dough from sticking.

Knead by hand for another 5 minutes. Grease a large glass bowl. Put dough inside and cover with tea towel. Place in warm area and allow to double in size, about 1 hour.

Punch down and divide dough into two equal parts. Place in greased loaf pans. Cover with tea towel and let rise until doubled in size.

Bake at 375 degrees for 25 minutes. Pull out and immediately take a stick of butter and rub over top of bread. Allow to cool on racks. Try not to eat both loaves in one sitting.

* * *

Don't have buttermilk? Because let's face it, sometimes the whim to bake hits when we're least prepared. But because we've got our pantry stocked, we can make a substitute for buttermilk by mixing in a tablespoon of lemon juice or apple cider vinegar to a cup of milk. Stir and let it sit for a few minutes. When the milk curdles and turns thick, you're ready to add it to your dough or batter.

***

If your kitchen is cool or you're not getting the rise you want, preheat your oven to 400°. Bake bread for 5 minutes before lowering the temperature to 375° and baking as directed. This trick works with any bread recipe as the extra heat kicks the yeast into overtime action.

Homemade Cornbread

There are two kinds of cornbread. Southern and not-southern. Southern cornbread is made without sugar and with white cornmeal. My grandmother was a true Southern lady and firmly stated yellow corn was for livestock and white corn was for humans. I use whatever cornmeal I have in the cupboard, but she was adamant about this.

If you want to make it Southern-style, omit the sugar.

Whichever way you make it, I promise you'll never want to go back to those little boxes of mixes.

½ cup butter
1½ cups all-purpose flour (may substitute 2 cups
    freshly ground spelt flour)
1 cup cornmeal
2 Tablespoons sugar
1½ Tablespoons baking powder
½ teaspoon baking soda
½ teaspoon salt
¼ cup coconut oil or lard
2 eggs
1 cup milk

Preheat oven to 350 degrees. Place ½ cup butter in 8x8 baking pan or 8-inch cast-iron skillet. Put in oven while it's preheating to melt the butter. Remove when butter is melted—this will grease the pan for you. If you happen to forget and butter turns brown and starts to boil, no worries. Just use a hot pad and pull out the pan when you remember or when you hear it popping in the oven...whichever comes first. One could use a timer, but life's more exciting in the kitchen without it.

In a large mixing bowl combine flour, baking powder, baking soda, salt, and cream of tartar. Cut in coconut oil. Add cornmeal. Stir in eggs, milk, and melted butter from skillet. Mix until just combined, but don't over-stir the batter.

Pour into greased pan. Place in oven and bake for 30 minutes or until center is set.

Homemade Tortillas

I don't know anyone who doesn't like tacos. My son is a picky eater, but if I wrap it in a tortilla, he's good to go.

However, a pack of eight tortillas can cost close to $5 at the store. Have you ever read the ingredient list on them? It's not so good.

Good news, tortillas are easy to make at home and cost a fraction of the price. I can make a batch of tortillas at home for less than a dollar.

The first time I made tortillas my husband was a bit skeptical. However, after the first bite he said, "These are so good you could sell them."

> **2 cups whole wheat flour**
> **1 teaspoon sea salt**
> **¼ teaspoon baking powder**
> **2 Tablespoons coconut oil or lard**
> **¾ cup warm water**

Measure out dry ingredients in a mixing bowl. Cut in the fat with a pastry cutter until it's absorbed into the flour. Pour in water and mix until it just holds together. If dough is too sticky, add a pinch more flour. If it's too dry, add a tablespoon of water at a time.

On a lightly floured surface, knead dough for 2 minutes. Cover and let rest for 20 minutes or longer. Resting the dough is important for the texture and rolling it out. You can skip it if you're in a hurry...totally been there, but truly, letting it rest will deliver a better tortilla. Mix the dough in the morning to save time on busy nights

Ready to roll?

Preheat a cast-iron skillet on medium heat. I usually preheat two so I can cook more tortillas at once.

Divide the dough out into eight balls. Lightly spread olive oil on your counter. Place the dough ball on the counter and push it down flat with the heel of your hand. With a rolling pin, roll out into a thin circle.

Place tortilla in heated cast-iron skillet. When small bubbles start to appear, flip the tortilla over. It will take approximately 2 minutes on each side. Have a tea towel or paper towel-lined large plastic bag ready to put hot tortillas into. This will help keep them pliable, and nothing is better than a fresh warm tortilla. I've been known to eat the first few before they even make it to the bag or towel.

Store cooked tortillas in the fridge if you have any left for another meal. You can also double the recipe if you have a large family or someone like me who likes to snitch a few extra tortillas before the meal is served.

* * *

I've used hard red wheat, hard white wheat, spelt, and mixtures in these tortillas. You can also use regular all-purpose flour, but we prefer the whole wheat in this recipe.

Trayer Wilderness Favorite Gluten-Free Bread Recipe

I've done a small amount of gluten-free baking but am in no way an expert at it. So I asked my good friend Tammy from TrayerWilderness.com to share her favorite gluten-free bread recipe with us. Tammy's family is strictly gluten-free, so I knew she'd have a well-tested recipe for us.

> 4½ cups warm water
>
> 2 Tablespoons (2 packages) active dry yeast
>
> ⅓ cup sucanat or organic sugar
>
> 1 Tablespoon salt
>
> 6 cups Better Batter flour (BetterBatter.org)
>
> 2 Tablespoons olive oil or melted butter

Mix sugar, water, yeast, salt, and olive oil and let set for 10 minutes to sponge.

Add flour two cups at a time and beat vigorously. Gluten-free flours need to be worked over hard. The dough will not be like regular wheat flour dough that you can handle. Use a spatula to transfer to two loaf pans. Wet your hands with warm water and press the dough into the pan as well as smooth the surface of the bread.

Let rise for an hour. Heat oven to 350 degrees and bake until surface is brown—roughly 30 to 40 minutes.

Homemade Yogurt

Making yogurt at home is easy, more frugal than the store, and yogurt can be used in almost any recipe in place of milk or mayonnaise. Did you know that yogurt made at home also contains more live cultures than store-bought because it's fresher?

You can use yogurt with a live culture in it from the store or order a starter online. There are many kinds of starters, even ones for dairy-free people! I purchased mine from CulturesForHealth.com.

Because I love all things heirloom, I went with heirloom Bulgarian yogurt starter. It's a sweeter flavor than Greek yogurt, making it more versatile in our home.

> **4 to 6 cups whole milk (do not use ultra-pasteurized, preferably non-homogenized as well)**
> **¼ cup yogurt (with live cultures) or yogurt starter**

Pour 4 to 6 cups of milk into a saucepan. On medium-low heat, bring the milk to 160 to 175 degrees. (A higher temperature will result in a thicker yogurt.) Keep at this heat for 15 minutes.

Allow milk to cool to 110 degrees. A layer of scalded milk will form on top. Skim this off with a spoon.

When milk reaches 110 degrees, pour into a clean glass Mason jar. Add starter and mix in thoroughly. Put a lid on your jar. Keep yogurt between 100 and 110 degrees for 4 to 6 hours. There are a few ways to do this. You can purchase a yogurt maker, but I prefer the more frugal route when possible. I've filled my slow cooker with three inches of water and turned it on the "keep warm" setting with the lid off. This setting keeps the water at 110 degrees. Another option is to wrap up your jars in a thick bath towel and put them in the oven. The oven works as a natural incubator. Both options work well. Just don't forget your yogurt is in the oven and turn it on!

After three to four hours check to see if yogurt is thick. Once it's reached the desired thickness, store in fridge for up to one week, if you don't gobble it up within a day or two.

If your yogurt separates too much with a lot of whey (watery liquid) on top, then your yogurt got a little too hot while fermenting. Try keeping it slightly cooler. You can either stir the whey back into the yogurt or drain it to use as liquid in cooking or fermenting.

Homemade yogurt isn't generally as thick as store-bought yogurt. My kids like really thick yogurt while I prefer mine creamier. If you want your yogurt to be thicker without straining off any of the whey, right before you put your yogurt into the fridge (while it's still warm) stir in a tablespoon of gelatin. Use 1 Tablespoon of gelatin per quart of yogurt. A whisk works well to avoid clumps of gelatin in the finished product.

Use yogurt in your smoothies, with fruit, in oatmeal, and in place of sour cream or mayonnaise in any recipe.

Make sure to save a ¼ cup of your fresh yogurt as your starter for your next batch. I freeze a ¼ cup of starter so I don't have to remember to save it later and so that the starter is at its strongest point, right after it's been fed.

✳ ✳ ✳

I recommend only using whole milk for everything. Whole milk has fewer sugars in it than skim or two-percent, which means less spike in blood sugar. Also, many of the vitamins in milk are contained in the fat. Plus, it just tastes better!

Homemade Bone Broth or Stock

Making your own stock or bone broth is an easy and frugal way to get more out of food you've already purchased. Purchasing a whole chicken or roast with the bone in is cheaper than purchasing the same amount of meat in boneless skinless or prime cuts.

We usually cook one whole chicken a week or other large bone-in cut of pork or beef. I can make several meals from that and then I take the leftover bones and make my own stock. These bones would have been thrown out, but by making my own stock or broth I'm stretching them even further. Bone broth also contains collagen and gelatin, which are nourishing for our bodies.

1 or 2 chicken carcasses or a few pounds of beef bones
¼ cup apple cider vinegar
onion, garlic, or other vegetable odds and ends
herbs of choice (I like rosemary, sage, thyme, oregano,
**   and basil)**
water

Place the carcass in the pot or slow cooker. Pour ¼ cup apple cider vinegar over the bones and let it sit for a half hour or so. Cover the carcass with water and bring to a boil. Then switch to a low simmer. Add vegetables and herbs.

I cook mine in the slow cooker for 12 to 24 hours or on top of our woodstove in a large stockpot. You can let it simmer for up to 48 hours—whichever suits you and your schedule.

When finished, pour through a fine-mesh sieve or cheesecloth. You can reuse the bones and make a second batch of stock if you wish. Discard cooked vegetables. Allow broth to cool and pour into clean Mason jars. Store in fridge for up to a week, freeze, or can it.

I use our homemade broth as a base for soups, gravies, and sauces and to cook quinoa or rice. It adds a depth of flavor and also vitamins and minerals.

Ham and Bean Soup

This is one of our favorite soups to use with your leftover ham bone. Best part, this frugal soup costs less than 55 cents a serving but doesn't skimp on taste. I've had both my husband and readers alike tell me this was the best soup they'd ever had.

1 ham bone with meat
1 cup diced onion
3 cloves garlic, chopped
1 cup diced carrot

1 cup chopped rutabaga (or parsnips)
1 cup sliced celery
4 cups white beans
4 cups water
dash of salt and pepper

Chop all of your vegetables up in fairly even size so they cook at the same rate. Put your ham bone in a large stock pot or Dutch oven. Dump in all your vegetables.

Add the beans (undrained if using canned, drained if you soaked dried beans the night before). Pour in 4 cups of water.

Bring to a low simmer on the stovetop. Allow to simmer for about 2 hours, stirring every now and then.

Once meat is falling off the bone, transfer bone to a plate. Using tongs, pick off any good chunks of meat remaining on the bone and put meat back into soup. Add a dash of pepper and salt. Serve.

If you want to make this soup in the slow cooker, cook on low for 3 to 4 hours. If you cook it too long in the slow cooker, it tends to lose the flavor from the vegetables and turn too mushy.

Homemade Refried Beans

Beans are a great way to stretch the budget. They're also extremely frugal. We love to eat these as is, in tortillas, with chips, and just about any way you can shovel them in.

I can up our shelled October beans in the fall just to make this on nights I'm pushed for time. (Many people know them as cranberry beans.)

You can also use dried beans and soak them before cooking. Place beans in a large bowl and cover them with warm water. Many people like to add a tablespoon of lemon juice or apple cider vinegar to the soaking water to help aid digestion. Let beans soak for up to twenty-four hours. Drain and rinse thoroughly.

1 Tablespoon olive oil, coconut oil, or lard
½ medium chopped onion
3 cloves minced garlic
2½ teaspoons chili powder (or more according to
   taste)
1 teaspoon garlic powder
1 teaspoon cumin
salt and pepper to taste
1 quart canned October beans (or 4 cups of any bean
   of your choice)
1 cup water or chicken broth

In a large saucepan over medium heat, place a tablespoon of olive, bacon grease, lard, or coconut oil and coat pan. The lard gives a true authentic taste.

Sauté onion for three minutes. Add garlic and spices and continue sautéing for one to two minutes.

Add beans to pot. I don't drain my home-canned beans. I only use a minimal amount of salt in canning and the juice in the can adds flavor on its own to recipes. If using store-bought beans, soak the night before, drain, and rinse. Add water or chicken broth. Bring to a simmer and cook for five minutes.

Mash beans with either an immersion blender or a potato masher. If beans have too much liquid, allow them to simmer with the lid off for a few minutes.

Hillbilly Beans

My son requested this recipe after coming home from the neighbors and seeing their dinner. He promptly named them Hillbilly beans.

1 pound ground beef
2 cups pinto or red beans

2 cups white beans
1 jar or 16 ounces tomato sauce
1 medium minced onion
4 cloves minced garlic
¼ cup molasses
3 Tablespoons brown sugar
¼ apple cider vinegar
2 teaspoons dry mustard
2 teaspoons salt

Soak your beans the night before. Drain after soaking. Place ground beef, onion, garlic, and beans in slow cooker. In a glass measuring cup mix together tomato sauce, molasses, brown sugar, vinegar, salt, and mustard. Pour over top of beef, beans, onion, and garlic. Liquid should just cover the beans and beef. Add more water if needed. Cook on low for 8 hours.

Taste before serving. If you like a stronger savory flavor, add a teaspoon of garlic and onion powder just before serving. You can also add a few pieces of bacon. I tend to think bacon makes everything taste better, but with the cost of bacon on the rise, it makes the dish more expensive.

These are wonderful served with corn bread, in a tortilla, or over nachos.

Sausage and Potato Soup

1 pound sausage
3 Tablespoons flour
2 cubed potatoes
½ of a medium onion, diced
3 cloves minced garlic
1 to 2 diced carrots
2 cups green beans
2 cups corn (optional)
3 cups broth or milk

salt and pepper to taste

3 coarsely chopped fresh sage leaves (optional)

In a large stockpot or Dutch oven brown the sausage, onion, and garlic over medium heat. Add in flour and stir until flour has absorbed the grease. Pour in your choice of liquid. I've oftentimes done half broth and half milk, or even all broth. Whisk until the liquid is incorporated with the flour mixture. Add in vegetables and bring to a low simmer. Simmer for a half hour or until vegetables are cooked all the way through.

Feel free to substitute any vegetable for another depending upon what you have on hand, what's in season, or your family's preferences.

The sausage gives the soup an out-of-this-world flavor. You might be tempted to lick your bowl clean.

Grandma's Chocolate Mayo Cake

Anyone else have a sweet tooth? I love to bake. Desserts are what make my kitchen go round. I used to purchase boxed cake mixes by the half dozen when they came on sale. Until (you guessed it) I started reading the ingredients.

I went back through our family recipes and came across my great-grandmother's chocolate cake recipe. This comes together super quick and tastes better than its processed boxed counterpart. After all, if a recipe has survived this many years, you know it has something going on.

The secret is the mayonnaise and the coffee. The coffee heightens the chocolate flavor and in my opinion, something can never taste too chocolatey. You don't taste the coffee in the finished cake.

2 cups flour (I use soft white wheat but all-purpose or cake flour is fine)

1 cup sugar

½ cup cocoa

1 teaspoon baking soda

1 teaspoon baking powder
¾ cup mayonnaise
1 egg (optional—use when making cupcakes)
½ cup cold water
½ cup brewed coffee
1 teaspoon vanilla

Preheat oven to 350 degrees. Stir all dry ingredients together. Combine wet ingredients with dry until smooth. Pour into greased and floured pans. Bake at 350 degrees for 30 to 40 minutes for a cake or 16 minutes for cupcakes. Cool completely before frosting.

Caramel Frosting

Homemade frosting is one of those things you'll never go back to the can for. The flavors, the options, the dive face-first into the bowl...

Frosting is pretty basic. You have the fat source, the sweetener, a liquid, and extracts or chocolate. Oh, but the flavors we can make.

This frosting gives a slight caramel flavor that pairs oh so nicely with chocolate. Is there anything that doesn't pair nicely with chocolate?

5 Tablespoons butter
1½ cups brown sugar
3 Tablespoons boiling water
1 teaspoon vanilla

Beat butter and slowly add in sugar until creamed together. Pour in boiling water and beat until creamy. Add vanilla. Spread over cooled cake or cupcakes.

Cream Cheese Frosting

I can't stand a frosting recipe that doesn't make enough to frost an entire cake. Or perhaps I use too much frosting...no, there's no such thing. This makes enough frosting to generously frost 18 cupcakes or a full-size cake.

> **8 ounces cream cheese, softened**
> **3½ cups powdered sugar**
> **½ cup butter, softened**
> **2 teaspoons vanilla**

Cream together all ingredients until smooth. If you don't have powdered sugar, simply run regular sugar through a blender or spice grinder for a finer texture.

Upside-Down Upright Apple Cake

If you're my husband, the only cake in the world needed is chocolate. However, I'm not that partial and happen to love all cakes. I especially love ones that create a lovely syrup in the bottom so I don't have to deal with frosting. Every girl needs a go-to cake when she's in a hurry. If you add fruit it makes it healthy, right?

I first made this cake for church. I intended it to be an upside-down apple cake, but I pulled it out of the oven right before we left for church and didn't have time to invert it. And the Upside-Down Upright Apple Cake was born.

> **½ cup coconut oil**
> **¾ cup brown sugar**
> **4 cups sliced apples, tossed in sugar and cinnamon**
> **2 cups all-purpose flour (or 2½ cups spelt flour or 1¾ cups pastry whole wheat flour)**
> **1 cup sugar**
> **2 teaspoons baking powder**
> **½ teaspoon cinnamon**

¼ teaspoon nutmeg
¼ teaspoon ginger
¼ teaspoon salt
2 eggs
1 cup buttermilk
2 teaspoons vanilla extract

Place coconut oil in a 9x13 pan and set in oven. Preheat oven to 350 degrees. Pull out pan when coconut oil is melted. Sprinkle brown sugar over the coconut oil. Spread apples out evenly in the pan. (You can use fresh or frozen apples. If frozen, thaw apples in fridge before using in cake.)

Mix together dry ingredients. Add in liquids and stir until just combined. Pour batter evenly over apples. Bake for 25 to 30 minutes or until a toothpick inserted into cake comes out clean.

Allow to cool. Invert or serve upright.

Grandma's Flaky Pastry

This is my great-grandmother's pastry and pie crust recipe. It is the best pie crust I've ever had. In fact, when I was little I wouldn't eat pie crust. Until we went to my great-grandmother's and I tasted hers. After my mother switched out her recipe to this one, I ate all of my pie crust.

I've even been known to roll out this pie crust, sprinkle it with cinnamon and sugar, and bake it without a filling. Yep, it's that good.

This recipe makes four 9-inch pie crusts.

4 cups all-purpose flour (if using spelt flour you'll
     need to increase this to 5 cups)
1¾ cups cold butter, lard, or coconut oil
1 Tablespoon sugar
2 teaspoons salt
1 Tablespoon apple cider vinegar

1 egg
½ cup very cold or ice water

Combine dry ingredients. Cut in butter, lard, or coconut oil. You can even use a mixture of the different fats. Add your egg and liquids, stirring until the dough just holds together. Do not overwork the dough.

Chill for at least 15 minutes.

Divide dough into four equal parts. Turn out onto a lightly floured surface or wax paper. Roll to ⅛-inch thickness. Bake with your favorite pie filling.

You can also freeze the dough. It thaws well in the fridge and will be nicely chilled for rolling out.

Note: Whichever fat you use, it's important that it be very cold. You get flaky pastry when the fat melts as it's baking, not when you're mixing. I've even used frozen butter and grated it on the largest hole on my grater.

Grandma's Apple Pasties

Nowadays we can have a fresh apple whenever we want. Almost all fruit is sold year-round in the aisle of our grocery stores. But when folks used to only eat what they'd put up themselves, they didn't always have apples to make a pie.

During the Great Depression my father's mother cooked with what they had on hand. The old gnarled trees of her orchard still stand sentinel in the fields of the old place at our family's homestead. Even when the apples in the barrels had been used up, the shelves still held applesauce. This recipe is how my grandmother would make apple pasties for a treat when the apples were all gone.

    2 flaky pastry crusts
    1 pint applesauce
    Lard or coconut oil for frying

Melt lard or coconut oil in a large cast-iron skillet over medium heat. Roll out two chilled pie crusts on a lightly floured surface. Using a biscuit cutter, cut out small circles of dough and spoon a few tablespoons of applesauce into the center. Place a top circle over it and with the tines of a fork, crimp the edges closed. Fry in hot oil until cooked, flipping over to cook each side.

Place cooked pasties on a towel and allow to cool before devouring. You can also sprinkle a dash of cinnamon and powdered sugar over the pasties when they come out of the oil.

From-Scratch Chicken Pot Pie

2 cups cooked, diced chicken or turkey (dark meat adds more flavor)

2 cups mixed vegetables (cooked or frozen)

½ cup diced onion

3 Tablespoons butter

2 Tablespoons flour

1 cup milk (can substitute chicken broth or, for a truly decadent treat, use cream)

¼ teaspoon salt dash of pepper

2 flaky pastry pie crusts

Preheat oven to 375 degrees. Roll out a pie crust and line bottom of pie plate. Melt butter in a saucepan over medium heat and cook diced onion until translucent, about 3 minutes. Stir in flour and form a paste. Slowly whisk in milk. Bring to a low simmer. Sauce will thicken as it cooks. If it's too thick, add more milk. If it's too thin, add another tablespoon of flour. You want a fairly thick sauce.

Add cooked poultry and vegetables to pastry lined pie plate. Pour sauce over vegetables and poultry. Place top pastry crust over the top. Crimp edges and cut slits in pie crust to allow venting. Place in preheated oven and cook for 45 minutes or until pie crust is golden.

Chapter 5

Clean

Finally, brothers and sisters, whatever is true, whatever
is noble, whatever is right, whatever is pure, whatever
is lovely, whatever is admirable—if anything is
excellent or praiseworthy—think about such things.

PHILIPPIANS 4:8

*Many of today's cleaning products, from what we use to clean our
homes to our bodies, contain dangerous chemicals. We shouldn't
have to worry about what we're using to clean things as much as
the item we're cleaning. I don't want my home or my life filled with
harmful things, including my cleaning cupboard.*

*The pioneers didn't have aisles of cleaning and personal care products to choose from. They used simple ingredients to meet all of their
cleaning needs, and you can too. I share easy recipes for every aspect
of your home.*

In high school I was hired to clean house for an elderly couple who lived up the road from us. I'm kind of surprised they hired me. I'd never kept house before and knew very little about cleaning.

One of the first tasks the wife gave me was to clean their oven. I didn't want to admit I'd never done this before in my life. Pride. Does it get you into trouble too?

I opened the oven door. Grease, boiled-over sauces, and burnt-on food greeted me. Obviously it was going to take more than a good wiping down with soap and water.

"You need the oven cleaner. It's in the cupboard under the kitchen sink." Was my inexperience so obvious?

I brought out a spray can of oven cleaner. Following the instructions for a cold oven, I sprayed the entire surface down and let it soak in. I lugged a vacuum cleaner through the house, running it over the carpets in every room.

I went back to the kitchen and with a roll of paper towels in hand, began to wipe down the oven interior. Black grime smeared the white towels and my hands. I scrubbed. And scrubbed. It seemed more ick bubbled up to replace what I'd just cleaned. A roll of towels later, I had a sparkling oven.

Happy to be done with the job, I headed back home. But as the day wore on, the skin on my hands started to burn. Red blotches scattered across the back of my hand and up my wrists.

I washed them but nothing seemed to take away the burning. Over the next few days my skin flaked and peeled. No amount of lotion soothed my raw skin.

My mom examined my sores. "Didn't you wear gloves when you cleaned the oven?"

I shook my head. "I didn't know you were supposed to. She just handed me the cleaner."

"I don't know why she didn't have you wear gloves. You shouldn't ever use oven cleaner without gloves."

Lesson learned. It took a week for my skin to heal.

In our homes and lives, there are so many dangerous things—and we don't realize the harm until the damage is done. We can wear gloves and hope we're protected, but we'd really be better off if we never came into contact with it all.

* * *

Each of us has our area of weakness. One of mine used to be all kinds of media. From the books I read, to the shows I watched, to the music I listened to. I realized I couldn't read books I wouldn't be willing to put my name on the cover of or watch TV shows I'd be embarrassed to talk about in church. Not just my spiritual life, but my everyday life was made better by these changes. What we come in contact with on a regular basis affects us, both in our spirit and in our health.

After I had children, my concern with all the chemicals used in our homes and lives really weighed on me. Walk down any cleaning aisle at a grocery store, and there are scores of different products all claiming to keep our homes clean. But upon closer inspection they're riddled with warnings and precautions. The list of what to do if they come in contact with your skin makes me question using them in the first place.

When my children were infants and learned to crawl, I suddenly reexamined my entire home from a different level. I crouched down and viewed my home from the floor. No dangling items remained, heavy things within grasp were removed, and the cleanliness of my floors mattered more.

Funny how changing our perspective makes a situation different. Just because I got down on the floor didn't change my house, it just put different things in front of my eyes.

I remembered how my hands had burned and hurt for days after using the oven cleaner. Typically, we don't walk around on our hands and knees. But babies have this neat habit of putting not just their hands in their mouth, but also their feet. This really got me to thinking. Did I want my children's sensitive skin to come in contact with these cleaners?

Nope. Nada, not one bit. Was I going to stop cleaning my home? No.

I began looking into natural cleaners. I knew my great-great-grandparents hadn't browsed the aisles at the general store for their favorite brand of cleaner. What had they used?

There are two natural ingredients most of us have already that can be used to clean just about every surface of our homes. You use them in your kitchen and your food on a frequent basis already.

Vinegar and baking soda. These two have become a staple in my home and cleaning closet. For cleaning, I usually use white vinegar, but I always have raw apple cider vinegar on hand for cooking and health reasons. Whichever you happen to have can be used. White vinegar is usually a bit cheaper, so I like to use it for cleaning. Here are some of my recipes for using vinegar and baking soda to clean.

* * *

The more attention I give to labels and ingredients lists, the more things I end up making at home.

From-Scratch Cleaning
Window Cleaner

Take a spray bottle, fill it a quarter of the way with vinegar, and then top off with water. I've used this cleaner with paper towels and washable rags, and it cleans my sliding glass door, the mirrors, and all the windows without a single streak. Now that my son is old enough to help with chores, I don't worry if he goes a little bit spray-happy or happens to get some on himself while cleaning.

Some people don't particularly like the scent of vinegar while cleaning. As it evaporates, the smell leaves, but if you want your cleaner to smell a little bit better, you'll want to try this next recipe.

Homemade Citrus All-Purpose Cleaner

4 to 5 citrus peels
3 cups white vinegar

Fill a quart-size canning jar three quarters full with your lemon peels. Pour white vinegar over the lemon peels. Let it set for a minute and then top off with more vinegar. Completely submerge the lemon peels. Cover with a lid and band and set in a dark cupboard for two weeks. Shake the jar every few days. You might want to mark the top of the lid with the date in case you forget.

In two weeks, pour the vinegar through a strainer or cheesecloth. Dilute with two parts water to one part lemon vinegar. Use on windows, countertops, mirrors, and as a general multipurpose cleaner. You can use any citrus fruit or add some herbs for your own unique custom blend.

If you don't have any citrus peels, you can add ten drops of your favorite lemon or orange essential oil.

Floor Cleaner

Ever notice small dark spots in the divots of your linoleum? Over time, soap builds up and dirt sticks to it. Using vinegar eliminates these spots. If you have little ones or pets, you won't have to worry about harsh chemicals where they play.

Add a cup or so of vinegar to your bucket or sink full of water. No soap. Use to mop your hardwood, laminate, tile, or linoleum. (It is not recommended to use acid-based cleaners, such as vinegar or citrus, on limestone and marble.)

Laundry

Add ¼ cup vinegar to your laundry instead of bleach. It will kill odor-causing bacteria and clean your washing machine with no discoloring. I toss mine into the liquid softener dispenser.

Drain Declogger

Vinegar is also an awesome way to unclog drains. Pour ⅛ to ¼ cup of baking soda down your drain. Follow it with a chaser of vinegar. I pour until it reaches a good foam, allow it to foam for a few seconds, and chase it again with more vinegar. Let your drain sit for ten to fifteen minutes. Pour a cup of boiling water down the drain. For an especially clogged drain, repeat. I do this every other month or so to keep pipes clear.

If you're having fruit fly troubles, this can clear up the problem. Fruit flies often lay eggs in your sink pipe. This will kill any eggs and help eliminate those pesky buggers. This past fall, I couldn't get rid of the fruit flies for anything. I set traps, locked up my fruit, and still had a few buzzing around. Within 24 hours of the baking soda and vinegar treatment, we were fruit fly free!

Carpet Cleaner

Dampen stains with the vinegar and water cleaner (test a small area first for discoloring). Blot up with a rag. If carpets have an odor, sprinkle baking soda over carpet, let sit for 15 minutes, and then vacuum.

Faucets

Wet a towel in vinegar. Wrap it around the faucet and handles and let sit for a half hour...or until you walk back in the room and remember you were cleaning, whichever comes first. Come back and wipe clean. Hard water stains and gunk will be gone.

Shower and Bathtub

I use baking soda to scrub the bottom of our shower and the tracks of our shower door. After rinsing off the baking soda, I spray all the surfaces with my vinegar rinse. I let it sit for a few minutes and then wipe clean.

Sinks

Sprinkle baking soda into your sink. Mix with a small amount of water to make a paste and scour the sink. It eliminates odor and rubs off stains. Rinse clean with warm water.

Toilets

Dump ½ cup baking soda into the toilet bowl. Let it sit for about fifteen minutes. Scrub with brush. This takes away any odor and scours off anything undesirable. Spray toilet seat, handle, and base with the homemade all-purpose citrus cleaner and wipe clean.

Dirty Dishes

Ever have baked-on food stuck in your pans? Liberally sprinkle on baking soda. Use the baking soda to scour off baked-on food. It absorbs the grease as you scrub. I've found this works best with a dry pan and no added water.

I use mostly cast iron for our cookware. Because soap can ruin a good seasoning, I use a salt scrub to remove cooked-on food. Sprinkle a few tablespoons of salt onto the cast iron and scrub. Dump soiled salt into the garbage and then rinse with hot water. Dry and lightly oil the cast iron before putting away.

Natural Oven Cleaner

Knowing firsthand what commercial oven cleaners can do to the skin, I was determined to never use them again. But when we were having Thanksgiving at our home, I couldn't leave my oven in its current state of messiness. Nothing makes me give my house a good cleaning like having company over. (I'm not sure if this means I should invite people over more often or clean my house more. Either way, I can get a month of Saturday cleanings done in a few hours if company is on the way.)

This method works extremely well and requires a small amount of elbow grease. Liberally sprinkle baking soda on the inside of your open oven door. Scrub with a dry rag or even your fingertip. It's safe and won't harm your skin. The dry baking soda absorbs the grease, and the grit lifts it off. I tried it with water, and it didn't work as well as the dry method for me. Especially soiled spots may need another dousing of baking soda.

Apply to the bottom of the oven. I did have to make a light paste with baking soda and water for the sides and top of the oven, but they usually don't have as much baked-on gunk. Use a small broom to sweep off the soiled dry baking soda.

Wipe any remaining residue with a damp cloth. You can also spray it down with your vinegar cleaner. Any spots that still have baking soda will foam.

I did try the foaming action to try and lift up the grease, but all it did was foam. It is fun for the kids to watch, but not so effective in getting the gunk up.

* * *

If you dedicate a little time each day to housekeeping, you'll stay on top of it. While I can't put in an hour every day, I can always find fifteen minutes. When truly focused, it's amazing what you can get done in just that short amount of time. I hate to leave dirty dishes on the kitchen counter. But some nights I'm so tired the thought of it makes me want to hurl them all into the garbage and use paper plates.

However, I can usually clean up those bowls and pots with five minutes of dedicated scrubbing. A lot of the time we build up a chore as taking much longer than it really does in our minds. Make a plan to put a little effort into housekeeping every day and see how much you can get done.

From-Scratch Body Care

After reading the ingredient labels (I may need to have this made into a shirt) on many of my skin care items, I ended up tossing almost all of them into the garbage. Here's what I use instead!

Homemade Lotion Bar

No matter what time of year, I tend to have really dry hands. In the winter months, the cold air seems to zap all moisture out. During the spring and summer months I've got my hands in the dirt pulling weeds, planting vege-tables, and gardening. It seems I can put lotion on five times a day and my skin is still dry.

Enter a lotion bar. For those of you who have never tried a lotion bar it is a hard form of moisturizer that, when warmed by the heat of your skin, melts just enough to rub in and be absorbed. Because of the beeswax, the moisture stays in the skin much longer than regular lotion.

As a bonus, it's extremely easy to make at home. And it doubles as lip balm.

> **beeswax**
> **coconut Oil**
> **shea Butter**
> **essential oil of lavender, lemongrass, or spearmint (optional)**

Using a food scale, weigh out equal amounts of beeswax, coconut oil, and shea butter. You'll have an easier time using beeswax pellets for measuring. If purchasing your beeswax from a local beekeeper, you'll most likely get a bar or chunk of beeswax, which makes it a tad bit harder for measuring, but still very doable. If you don't have a local source for beeswax, I've used MountainRoseHerbs.com for my ingredients.

I use one and a quarter ounces of beeswax, coconut oil, and shea butter for a decent-sized batch. Using a double boiler or a small saucepan and a large glass bowl, melt beeswax, coconut oil, and shea butter until it turns to a liquid. Remove from heat and add ten drops of essential oil. Note: Make sure if you use essential oils in the recipe that the essential oils you use are of high quality and are safe for external use on the skin.

Pour into molds. You can use soap molds, silicone cupcake liners, or even fill a small parchment paper-lined box. I used a plastic lid from a box of oval candles. The size just fits the palm of your hand. Whatever mold you use, make sure it's something you can easily pop the hardened bars out of. Allow bars to harden overnight.

Wipe out your measuring bowl while it's still warm for easier cleaning and then wash with hot soapy water. I use the small amount of the lotion bars still clinging to the inside of the bowl to rub on my feet and elbows. Be sure to put socks on as the soles of your feet will be slippery until the lotion is completely absorbed. Let's say I learned that one the hard way...

You can also use this same recipe for lip balm. Pour into smaller containers or empty twist-up lip balm tubes.

All-Purpose Soothing Salve

To make this salve, you'll need to plan ahead by about 4 to 8 weeks in order to make the calendula-infused olive oil. Fill a pint-sized Mason jar about ⅔ full with dried calendula blossoms. Cover blossoms with olive oil, put a lid on it, and set on a sunny windowsill. Swirl and shake jar every few days as the calendula infuses the olive oil. After a minimum of 4 weeks, strain oil into a clean jar and use in homemade recipes. Note: Always use dried herbs when infusing to avoid excess moisture and the introduction of mold.

> **1 ounce coconut oil**
> **1 ounce shea butter**
> **1 ounce beeswax**
> **1 ounce calendula-infused olive oil**

Over a double boiler, melt coconut oil, beeswax, and shea butter. Remove from heat and stir in calendula-infused olive oil. Pour into clean 6-ounce wide-mouth Mason jar and allow to cool. Use as a soothing salve or moisturizer for rough, dry skin on elbows and feet.

From-Scratch Sugar Body Scrub

I'm the type of gardener who doesn't wear gloves. I like the feel of dirt sifting between my fingers and getting my hands dirty as I tend to my plants. But I don't like the stain of dirt in the lines of my skin or around my fingernails after a few hours of digging in the garden.

Sometimes soap and water don't get into all the little crevices. Not to mention, dirt is especially drying. This is my favorite scrub as it exfoliates and gets the dirt out, plus it moisturizes better than any other store-bought option I've tried. Best part, you already have all the ingredients hiding in your kitchen cupboard.

A wide-mouth six-ounce Mason jar works best. You can use a narrow mouth, but it makes it hard to fit your hand in to scoop out the scrub. Smaller batches and jars work better as the oil can go rancid if you let the scrub sit for months on end. If you want to use a different-sized jar or make up one large batch to divide up into gifts, just use equal amounts of oil and sugar.

> ¼ cup sugar
> ¼ cup olive oil

> **Scent options:**
> 3 to 4 drops favorite essential oil
> ¼ teaspoon cinnamon and nutmeg
> 1 Tablespoon coffee grounds

Measure ingredients into a bowl and mix until well combined. Adjust scent options to your preference. Scoop sugar scrub into your preferred jar.

To use, scoop a small amount into your hand and scrub over skin. Rinse with warm water. If using in the shower, be careful as it can be a bit slippery, especially when using it on the feet. I also go barefoot in the garden so I end up using quite a bit of this scrub in the summer months.

Bentonite Herbal Facial Scrub/Mask

¾ cup old-fashioned oatmeal, ground fine
¼ cup dried lavender buds, ground fine
½ cup dried calendula, ground fine
1 Tablespoon ground flaxseed
½ cup bentonite clay

In a grinder or food processor, grind oatmeal, lavender buds, calendula, and flaxseed. In a glass container mix the ground ingredients well with the bentonite clay. Don't use metal with the bentonite clay as it will make the bentonite clay less effective.

You may use as a scrub or a mask.

For a scrub: If you have oily or acne-prone skin, mix 1 teaspoon scrub with 1 teaspoon water to make a paste. If you have dry skin, mix 1 teaspoon scrub with 1 teaspoon olive oil. With fingertips, lightly scrub face. Rinse with warm water.

For mask application: Mix 1 teaspoon of the dry mask with ¾ teaspoon apple cider vinegar and ¾ teaspoon water. The apple cider vinegar will help the bentonite clay mix better. Using your fingers, spread the mask evenly over your face, avoiding the eye area and lips. This will be enough to do your whole face.

Leave on for 5 to 20 minutes. As it dries your skin will begin to feel sort of tingly, and it might feel tight when you smile. Rinse off with warm water. Don't be alarmed if your skin is red after washing it off. It will fade after a few minutes.

Homemade Hair Rinse and Scalp Treatment

Apple cider vinegar is wonderful for many things, including your skin and hair. It will help remove buildup on your hair, leaving it shiny when used as a rinse. And don't worry—once your hair dries, it won't smell like vinegar.

**½ cup apple cider vinegar
2 cups water
essential oils or herbs (optional)**

Mix vinegar with water and any optional scent options. After shampooing, pour the vinegar mixture onto your hair and scalp. Let sit for a few minutes and rinse. Use a spray of cold water to up the shine factor. See how your hair does with the vinegar, adjusting how often you use it as your hair reacts. Try once a week and go from there.

Homemade Moisturizing Hair Mask

Winter can suck the moisture from hair, while summer months of swimming and harsh sunlight can also cause dry hair. Sometimes a girl just needs more than a regular conditioner or vinegar rinse.

**¼ cup calendula infused olive oil, regular olive oil, or
melted coconut oil**

Work the oil into your hair, paying special attention to the ends. Wear an old shirt as oil can stain. I take an old ponytail holder and pile it on top of my head. If company happens to come by, just tell them you're in the middle of a spa treatment or they might wonder why your hair is so oily looking. Leave on your hair for 15 to 30 minutes. Shampoo as normal. Use whenever your hair feels especially dry.

Homemade Face Moisturizer

As someone with acne-prone skin, I used to worry about using anything on my face with the word oil in it. However, jojoba oil contains similar properties to sebum (the oil produced by our bodies), so our skin doesn't react to it like other oils. It also has many vitamins in it that nourish the skin and combat aging. After researching parabens and other common ingredients in commercial moisturizers, I found using jojoba oil was the most frugal yet still effective option for me, and perhaps you will too.

organic cold-pressed jojoba oil
essential oil (optional)

I use about 5 drops of jojoba oil straight on my face as a moisturizer and as an eye makeup remover. I'll place the jojoba oil in my hand, add a drop of my favorite essential oil for skin, and then apply.

As you go about your day, I hope you remember to be careful with what you come in contact with both physically and spiritually. Be sure you're protecting yourself from harmful things.

Chapter 6

Prepare

Keep your lives free from the love of money and be
content with what you have, because God has said,
"Never will I leave you; never will I forsake you."

HEBREWS 13:5

It's not a matter of if hardships will come, but when. If we're prepared ahead of time, we'll be able to face these times and not only survive, but come out stronger for them.

Many times we think of one area of our life in being prepared. This chapter walks us through how our faith plays the biggest part and shares tips for getting your finances in shape, building up a food supply, and focusing on what's really important. Simple tips aren't always easy, but they are doable. Read on to see how you can begin today.

I enjoy walking out to our mailbox at the end of our driveway. There's a little thrill in not knowing what might come. A new magazine, a book, a letter from a friend. There's some mail I simply can't wait to open until I get to the house. I rip it open, juggling the other pieces, to read as I walk back up the gravel driveway.

Much as I love to get the mail, I don't always get pieces of mail I love. Like bills. Credit card statements.

Especially credit card statements.

My father has never in his life had a credit card. He grew up in a time and belief if you didn't have the money to pay for it, you didn't buy it. Wise advice. Needed advice. Advice sadly lacking in today's mainstream society and mindset.

One thing I don't do is carry a credit card balance. I pay off our credit card bill in full every month and use the card for the reward benefits. But some months those extra expenses creep up on me.

The brakes went out on our truck. The treads on our car tires were worn down smoother than petals on my spring rosebuds. The insurance didn't cover dental work and we didn't find out until after the work had been done.

Each month an unplanned and unexpected bill came up. Each month I put it on our credit card and then paid it off in full. Each month I had to take money out of our savings account in order to do this.

All of those *each months* add up, let me tell you. I sat down to pay the bills and realized we had very little money left in our savings account. Those months had taken a toll. I'd been taking money out and never putting any back in.

I knew this had been happening, but I hadn't really taken a look at the numbers in black and white. When they're staring you in the face on paper, it's a little bit harder to ignore than imaginary columns in your mind.

You can't stick to a budget if you never bother to make one.

I know what our set monthly bills are and I know what we bring home in our paychecks. But I'd never done the math all the way out to see how much we had left over after paying our regular bills each month. I was kind of doing a guestimate.

Here's the problem. My guestimating wasn't so hot. Hence the almost-depleted savings account.

When you realize you're one month away from not having any kind of fallback at all, it can hit you like the smell of a fish forgotten in a cooler during the hottest part of August. In case you've never experienced said smell, it can literally make your knees buckle, your eyes water, and your gag reflex go into overdrive simultaneously.

I realized we could keep on this path, or we could sit down and come up with a plan. If you're serious about getting your finances in order you have to write it out. You can use a spreadsheet, computer program, or a piece of notebook paper like I did, but bottom line is you have to write it out.

In doing this I learned some important things. One, it wasn't just the big unexpected expenses that were getting us. It was the little every week purchases that were adding up too.

We divided up our leftover funds after the regular bills were paid by the four weeks in a month. This was how much we could spend without taking money from savings. And if we wanted to put money into savings, we had to spend less than that amount. Sounds easy, right?

Second week in we totally blew it. Those old habits die hard. Really hard.

When we mess up, it doesn't mean we should give up. Too many times I've made mistakes and tossed my hands in the air. "See, I told you I couldn't do this. I proved you right." And back into my tangled-up hog pen of sin I go.

It's easy to give up. It's easy to quit fighting the fight and go back into what we know.

Watch and pray so that you will not fall into temptation.
The spirit is willing, but the flesh is weak (Matthew 26:41).

When this happens it's because I'm trying to change on my own. I
want my determination and will to be enough. If I say I'm going to do
something and try, then everything should fall into place. But sometimes, no matter how much effort we put into things on our end, we
still end up failing. We have a moment of weakness and our same old
habits and patterns blow in like a Northeastern blizzard in the middle of January.

When I completely overspent the second week, I wanted to say, *This
is too hard. There's no way we can get by on this amount every week.*

But when I trust, I'm given a beautiful gift. My shoulders aren't
weighed down. I realize the only job I have is to obey God. The rest is
up to Him. He is much more capable than you or I.

While we do need to keep an eye on our earthly bank account, we
also have a faith account. There have been many times in my life where
I continually draw out of my Jesus fund without ever replenishing it.
When we don't nurture that relationship, we suffer for it, because when
we're not close to Him, we tend to make bad decisions.

Remain in me, as I also remain in you. No branch can bear
fruit by itself; it must remain in the vine. Neither can you
bear fruit unless you remain in me (John 15:4).

As for that earthly account, I've learned a few things to help you
there as well.

Many people think *frugal* means *cheap*. There is a difference. When
I first started out in my own home with my husband, I wanted to purchase the cheapest of everything. When we bought a lawnmower, we
purchased the very cheapest push model available. It lasted one season.

I tend to be a creature of habit, so what did I do? I went and bought
another cheapest-of-the-line lawnmower. It also lasted one season. We
tried to take it to a repair shop, but by the time all of the parts were
replaced, it was actually cheaper to purchase a new one. Thankfully, I
do learn, even if it takes me a few tries.

This time, I purchased the best model we could afford. It's now been over eight years and it's still running fine. Moral of the story: The cheapest route is not always the most frugal route. I've found it's better to invest in a quality item than it is to buy cheaper ones that don't last as long. However, don't use this as an excuse to buy only the best of popular brand names. Research what others are saying about the item you're considering.

Like I mentioned early, you need to have a budget written out. Because not all of our bills are monthly, I went back at least three months (a year on our power bill) and averaged out any bills that don't occur monthly, to be prorated in our monthly budget. For example, our power bill comes every other month, but it greatly varies from the winter months to the summer months. I added the whole year's power bills together and then divided it out by twelve. You'll need to go through past bank statements or credit card statements to make sure you catch all of these. Don't forget to include tithing or other forms of charity giving in your budget.

Finally, I wrote down how much money we have coming in each month. I did not count in our tax refund or any bonuses as these aren't a guaranteed source of income. Once you've done all this, you'll see how much money you have left to spend on groceries, entertainment, gifts, and adding to your savings account. Let me say it's a bit different to see that number in black and white on your paper than as a guesstimate floating about in your head.

In order to save money, I needed to reduce the amount of some of our bills. I'll share some of the tips, tricks, and ways we use to reduce our monthly bills, but the biggest battle you'll face is changing your mindset.

We are conditioned as a society to think we need things in order to have the perfect life and to be happy. This is the mindset that gets us into trouble. We truthfully need very little in order to live. A frugal mindset makes us appreciate what we have more, though there are times when this is hard. When another unexpected bill comes and I have no idea how we're going to pay it, my faith walk gets real and I have to put on my hiking boots. I have to choose to believe God is also the God of my finances and will provide a way.

Look at the birds of the air; they do not sow or reap or store away in barns, and yet your heavenly Father feeds them. Are you not much more valuable than they? Can any one of you by worrying add a single hour to your life? (Matthew 6:26-27).

What We Buy

Instead of buying your groceries for foods and dishes you want, use the food already in your pantry to create meals. By learning to cook from scratch, you'll be surprised at how many things you can make from basic ingredients. Go through the food you already have in your home and come up with a menu for the week. When you go to the store, only purchase the items you have to have in order to complete the meal.

I know this seems basic, but you'll be surprised at how much money it saves.

Too often our purchases are made by what we want, not by what we need. I'm not saying you can't ever buy anything you want, but if you're struggling to make ends meet you need to reevaluate what you're spending your money on.

I like clothes. Despite being a homesteading mama, I get excited over a new top, cute pair of pants, or vintage style dress. Even though I shop from the clearance racks and thrift stores, I could easily fill my closet twice over if given the chance. But I've learned most of the time I don't need those clothes. Many times I'm getting rid of a piece of clothing because I no longer like it, not because it's worn out. Learning to wear clothes until they're actually worn out is a frugal lesson our ancestors knew. Sometimes a seam rips, a button falls off, the hemline is too long, or we lose weight. Simple sewing skills can transform a piece of clothing into something you like again.

If we truly evaluate our purchases, most of the things we buy are wants, not needs. Learning to tell the difference will make a huge difference in how you spend your money.

7 Ways to Live Like Laura Ingalls

1. **Cook from scratch.** It's amazing how many folks don't know how to make things from scratch, and I used to be one of them. I used to rely on canned cream-of-something soups, packets of this and that, and premade mixes, and then I realized it is way more frugal and tastier to make food at home. Don't be overwhelmed by making things from scratch. Pick one item you usually purchase from the store and focus on making that yourself until it's part of your normal routine. Then add the next item.

2. **Grow a garden.** Use the tips from chapter 1 to begin growing some type of food at your home.

3. **Preserve your own food.** You may not be able to grow it all, but what you do grow and what you get from other sources should be preserved for future eating. There are many ways to preserve food at home from freezing, canning, dehydrating, fermenting, root cellar, and even in alcohol or oil.

4. **Stock the basics.** When Laura and Pa went to town for supplies, they didn't grab this or that and have aisle upon aisles of food to pick from. They stocked basic items they could make multiple meals from like salt, oats, sugar, and coffee. If you have the basics in stock it will be much easier to make your meals from scratch. You won't have to run to the store every time you want to cook. That can get costly and make you less likely to cook due to the hassle.

5. **Be able to start a fire anywhere.** A fire can be the difference between life and death. Fire was and is

important for cooking, keeping warm, and providing light.

6. **Wear an apron.** An apron has many functions. First, it protects your clothes! The pioneers often only had two or three dresses, and an apron kept them from wearing out as quickly and needing extra washing. Perhaps I'm the only cook who manages to splatter grease or sprinkle flour all over the kitchen like the good fairy. Most aprons have pockets, which can be used to hold extra ingredients or measuring spoons. An apron can also be used as a potholder to protect hands from burns.

7. **Have faith.** A Bible was often the only book a family had. Scripture's words of wisdom and God's love were what kept many a family going. When crops failed and hardships arose, their faith was buoyed by the everlasting promises of Jesus. The real treasure isn't in how much money we have, how well-off we are, or our comfort level. It's in leaning on Jesus and seeing ourselves and this world through His eyes.

Household Tips

What follows are ways I save money in our household. By saving money I can then apply it toward our debt or to those items I truly do need. Most of my tips seem small, but they add up. And small things are doable and don't freak us out as much, which is good when we're trying to make lasting changes.

Laundry

Wash clothes in cold water. If they're really grimy, you may want to use warm water. For most loads, cold water works fine. I promise you, we don't go around with dirty, stinky clothes.

Use a clothesline or drying rack. During the good-weather months, I use a clothesline. This cuts down my power bill by at least fifty dollars per billing cycle. If you can't string a clothesline, then try using a drying rack. Plus, there's something about hanging up each article of clothing that soothes me. I often times say a prayer for the wearer of each garment.

Drying racks can be used no matter what the outside weather is doing or if you have strict homeowner's association rules. I would invest in a sturdy stainless steel drying rack. Wooden ones can stain your clothes when the wood gets wet, and the glue tends to weaken and allow the rods to fall out of place.

Have you ever noticed when you hang your clothes out to dry you don't have any lint traps to clean? This is because the dryer wears your clothes out faster. The lint you clean out is fibers from your clothing, causing more wear and tear than if they'd dried on the line or rack.

I also advise making your own laundry detergent. You're probably wondering if it really cleans the clothes and if it's cheaper than store-bought. Yes to both. Our clothes never smell funny (unless I left them wet too long in the washer and had to rewash them, which is not frugal at all, but happens occasionally), the dirt and grime washed out the same as with store-bought detergent, and it only cost $4.50 for three gallons of soap.

Much cheaper by far. Good news, it only takes about fifteen minutes to whip up a batch for a six-month supply of detergent. Of course, this will vary depending upon how much laundry you're washing.

Below is my mom's recipe. We went grocery shopping together and she saw me reach for a bottle of laundry detergent on the shelf. "It's a lot cheaper to make it," she said.

My hand hovered over the bottle. "I know, but doesn't it take forever? I only have a day's worth of soap left at home and I have to work tomorrow."

"You just boil water and stir it together. It's pretty fast."

I wavered.

"I'll come down and do it with you."

My mom's good at countering my excuses, no matter how old I get. "Deal."

True to her word, she came down and we whipped up three gallons of soap in less than half an hour. I've been hooked ever since.

Homemade Liquid Laundry Detergent

> 4-ounce bar of soap, grated (I chose a natural soap scented with lemon)
> 4 cups of boiling water
> 2½ gallons of hot water
> 1 cup Borax
> 1 cup washing soda (not to be confused with baking soda)
> ½ cup Oxyclean or powdered bleach that says it's safe for colored clothes (optional, but more stain-fighting power)
> ¼ cup baking soda
> 20 to 30 drops essential oil (optional)

Find yourself a big pot or bucket. I used a five-gallon bucket to mix up my soap. Grate your soap into your bucket. Add 4 cups boiling water. Stir until all of this is dissolved. Hot tap water doesn't dissolve the soap or the powders enough. You may wish to wear gloves to prevent burns from the hot liquid.

Add the rest of the hot water, Borax, washing soda, powdered bleach, and baking soda. Stir until all is dissolved. It will be kind of goopy. Add the essential oils after everything else is dissolved and mix well. Let it sit overnight, stirring occasionally as you remember. I leave it in the corner of the kitchen so I'll be sure to see it and stir.

I kept some of the soap in the bucket with a lid on, but I poured some into half-gallon wide-mouth Mason jars to keep above the washer for easier dispensing. I tell you what, everything just looks better in a Mason jar. It's my number-one decorating go-to.

Use ⅓ to ½ cup per load. It doesn't suds up like commercial soap, so don't be worried you did something wrong if you don't see suds. This kind of threw me the first few times I used it as I was used to the suds, but it doesn't affect the cleaning ability.

The main cost of the soap is the bar of soap as the other ingredients cover multiple batches. I chose a handmade lemon-scented bar from our local co-op as I wanted the detergent to be as natural as possible, but still smell good. I got my powdered bleach at the dollar store. The other items can be found on the laundry detergent aisle of most grocery stores or online.

Energy Use

Unplug items not in use. You know how you can walk through your home in the middle of the night and see all kinds of green, red, and blue appliance lights blinking at you? Those glowing lights are all drawing power. I put all the electronics at my desk and in our family room on a power strip. Whenever they're not in use, I flip off the power strip, eliminating phantom power.

Reuse items. So many things can be used again and again. I rinse out plastic storage and freezer bags and dry them to use later. Butter wrappers are excellent to use for greasing a pan. Cut up old towels into cleaning rags or use old socks as a cleaning mitt. Parchment paper is one of my favorite baking tools. I can reuse the same piece of parchment paper to bake bread up to five times. Almost anything in our homes can be put to another purpose!

Run things during non-peak hours. Most power companies charge a different rate per hour during non-peak and peak hours. I try to run our dishwasher, washing machine, and dryer (when weather inhibits the clothesline) during non-peak hours. Non-peak hours are often from 8:00 a.m. to 8:00 p.m., excluding weekends. Contact your power company for exact hours and rates.

Check your thermostat. Last time the power went out, it somehow reset our thermostat. I got quite a shock when our electric bill came. Now I check it frequently. Just a couple of degrees can make a big difference. My husband is a sawyer so we have access to firewood. With the frequent power outages, we heat our home with a wood-burning stove. My electric heat only comes on if it gets below 56 degrees in the house...usually never.

Shopping

There are a few things I've learned when I'm tempted to go on a spending splurge or I'm standing in the store with a cart filled with items that jumped off the shelves into it. I do my best to only go shopping once a month for the main part of our groceries. If I'm not in the stores I'm not as tempted.

If I simply can't walk away from something, I'll leave it in the bag with the receipt for a week or so. If I haven't used it in that amount of time, I'll reevaluate if I needed it or simply wanted it. Many times I end up taking it back.

Shopping online is another temptation. It's so easy to put something into that virtual cart. I'll put things into the cart and not complete the order for a day or two. If I go back to the website and cart and find I still think it's a wise purchase, I'll make it. Otherwise I hit delete and leave the site.

Another pitfall I used to fall into is the good deal bargain mindset. If it's 65 percent off, how can I pass up those kinds of savings?

It's still spending money. If it's an item you need, then that's great, but many times it's just the good deal that snags me.

Remember this earth is not our home. It is so easy to want to fill our emptiness with *things*. But these things, no matter how many we incur or how big and bright they are, can never fill us up like the love of Jesus. We can be surrounded by a mountain of things and feel alone and unsatisfied. But we can have nothing but the love and peace of Jesus and be satisfied for eternity.

8 Foods to Store at Home

Our goal is to have close to a year's supply of our staples on hand. These are the eight foods I believe you should be storing. I don't include fruits and vegetables as most of us can grow or harvest these at home or close to our homes.

1. **Salt** can be used to preserve food as well as flavoring dishes. I put salt at the top of the list because most of us don't have a way to get salt where we live. We can all grow our own herbs, but most people do not have a naturally occurring salt source in the vicinity of their home. Store salt in a dry area as moisture will make it cake together.

2. **Fat source.** Fruits and vegetables are part of a well-balanced diet, but our bodies require a certain amount of fat in order to function. We need fat for cooking and baking. I use butter, lard, coconut oil, and olive oil. Keep your fat source out of the heat and light. I put extra butter and lard in the freezer.

3. **Wheat berries.** You'll see flour on lots of food storage lists, but quite frankly, flour is not meant for long-term storage. It will go rancid and can also be a home for pests. Wheat berries and other forms of grain will store for years. Not only can they be ground into flour, but they can also be soaked and cooked into a cereal. We use about 100 pounds of wheat berries a year. I use hard white wheat and spelt as our primary type of wheat berries. Store wheat berries in a cool and dry location.

4. **Honey** is a nonperishable food. Raw honey is excellent for eating, cooking, and medicinal purposes. You can make a ginger-infused honey for medicinal purposes during cold and flu season. Honey is also excellent for

baking. If honey hardens or forms crystals, simply place it in hot water. Plus, honey just plain tastes good. I love to swirl it in my coffee. Store honey out of direct sunlight.

5. **Sugar** is needed in baking and also canning homemade jams and jellies. However, I don't use regular processed white sugar. I use organic evaporated cane sugar, and all of my jam and jelly recipes use about a quarter of the sugar most recipes call for. Store sugar in a dry place in a pest-proof container.

6. **Dried beans** are not only inexpensive and easy to store, but they have huge nutritional value. Beans can be used in multiple dishes and should be stored in a dark, cool, and dry place.

7. **Oatmeal** is inexpensive and can be used for cereal, in baked goods, or even ground up into flour. It contains fiber and is easy to flavor with seasonal fruits and spices. We have oatmeal for breakfast at least once a week, if not more. Cinnamon, a pat of butter, and a smidgen of sugar is excellent. We add peaches, blueberries, raisins, and other fruits as they come into season. Store oatmeal in a dry place.

8. **Coffee.** Most of us do not have a source of coffee available to us other than purchasing it. If you're a tea drinker, then stock up on your teas. But I am a coffee lover. While we could live without coffee, I'd rather have it on hand. Does anyone else just open the canister of coffee and take a big whiff? Whole coffee beans will store much longer than ground coffee and should be stored in a dry and dark area.

Dreams and Realities

I cook on our woodstove during the winter months. With a cast-iron Dutch oven, I can fry meat and simmer a stew or soup without drawing any electricity. Best part, I get to pretend I'm Laura Ingalls Wilder.

I grew up in a singlewide 1974 trailer, a far cry from Laura's cabin in the big woods. Windows sweated, and there was just enough space between my twin bed and the closet to hold a small dresser. When the cold Northeastern wind roared its way through the mountain passes into our valley, the whole house trembled. In the middle of summer, it filled with heat until you could almost see heatwaves shimmering off the walls.

I dreamed of having a house with a staircase and a real fireplace with a mantel. We had a small woodstove sandwiched between the kitchen and the living room. It heated the house quickly, but the minute it went out, cold air filtered through the thin windows.

Thankfully, my father was a logger and we always had a large pile of firewood spread out beneath the towering fir tree just off the front porch. Its large evergreen branches provided a canopy, stretching out some thirty feet, from the worst of the snow and rain.

A small part of me was embarrassed to have people find out I lived in a trailer once I hit my teenage years. I chose to walk home in the dark and cold from the end of the road rather than get off the school bus at our trailer. Looking back, I want to give the younger me a hug and say it doesn't matter what kind of house I lived in, I was lucky to have a home with electricity, water, and heat. Oh, hindsight.

Despite this knowledge, the dream of a built home called to me. A renovated farmhouse with a wooden curved banister running up a flight of stairs and real oak floors leading to a river rock fireplace were the things my daydreams were made of. I wanted a large wooden barn, complete with a hay mow and stalls filled with horses and a milk cow. Maybe a stainless steel milking room. The kitchen, oh the kitchen, with a large farmhouse sink and walk-in pantry lined with shelves sturdy enough to hold all our home-canned goods and equipment.

My husband and I purchased our acreage and a manufactured home when my son was a year old. The property once belonged to my grandfather, the same one who'd brought his family out from North Carolina. He died before I was born, but owning the land he did makes me feel connected. When we were able to purchase it and keep it in the family, my heart warmed. I've never had any desire to move beyond our little gravel road at the base of the mountain that's stood sentinel over every season of my life so far.

My roots go deep here.

Still, I find myself peeking at homes for sale near where we live. I imagine the floor plan I'd choose if we could build anything we wanted in the place of our current home. And I love to watch those home renovation shows on television. The before-and-after shots are almost too incredible to believe. What once was stained, out of date, broken, and ugly is transformed into a work of art. Granite countertops gleam next to polished stainless steel. Even the closets have chandeliers and the dog a custom-made bed.

My gaze roves over my home. Wouldn't marble or granite look better than the tile-wrapped Formica I have?

Hardwood floors. Real hardwood floors. I've been known to drool over hardwood floors. It might be because I'm a logger's daughter and a sawyer's wife, but whatever the case, I love real wood. It heats our home, it shelters my head, and each variety is unique. The subtle differences in density, the flavors for smoked meat, the grain and colors once cut, the way it grows tall and provides shade in the summer and a wind break in the winter. I've lingered over almost all types of wood, imagining which kind I'd like to put down on my living room floor. Being an old-fashioned gal, I always like the wood found in old homes the best. You can't find the grain and charm of those floors that have witnessed years of life on the shelf in a store.

Everywhere we turn, we can find ideas and ways to change our homes. I gaze at the pictures worthy of gracing a magazine with everything neatly tucked into places, surfaces gleaming, and my heart begins to yearn for things beyond what I have.

When I passed a *For Sale* sign on my way home from work one day, I eyed the price and the pictures posted of the inside of the home.

I felt God whisper to me, "Why do you long for these things? These are nothing compared with the mansion I'm building for you in heaven. Nothing can compare with what awaits you up here."

I sat at the stop sign, my blinker clicking. Windshield wipers flicked the raindrops away. I'd known this in my head for years. But it wasn't until that moment I knew it in my heart.

You see, the main problem with our overspending and breaking budgets isn't money. It's trying to fill a need inside ourselves with things instead of God's presence and love.

I'm not saying we can't have nice homes, we can't buy new things, or desire to make home improvements, but when these become something that overtakes us and becomes a priority that endangers our bank account, then we have a problem. When our hearts want more worldly things than Jesus things, we have a deficit.

We need a heart and soul transformation. Those before-and-after shows are a visual of what Jesus does to our lives when we invite Him in. He takes our stained, broken, damaged places and within the breath of asking Him into our hearts and lives, washes it all away. He transforms us into works of art. Works of art that will never tarnish and never go out of style or date.

> Do not love the world or anything in the world. If anyone loves the world, love for the Father is not in them (1 John 2:15).

When we focus on Jesus and the things of heaven, suddenly the new things don't matter so much.

Chapter 7

Livestock

I am the good shepherd. The good shepherd
lays down his life for the sheep.

JOHN 10:11

Raising any animal teaches you a lot about yourself. The Bible verses about shepherding take on a whole new level of meaning when you've actually experienced taking care of a flock! Raising animals has taught me many an important faith lesson.

While raising livestock is work—and harder for some, depending upon your location—most folks, even those in an urban setting, can raise some type of livestock. I share tips and considerations on choosing livestock, frugal options and ways to cut down on feed bills, and how you can incorporate raising livestock into your life and home.

If you ever see a woman chasing a chicken with a sheet in a yard, don't think she's gone crazy. You may offer to help, or you may sit back and watch the show. Either way, you'll be highly entertained.

Our small flock of chickens has been one of the most interesting homesteading undertakings we've taken. This spring my strawberries were almost ripe. Glistening red berries dripped over the side of the cedar planter boxes. I planned on picking them with my kids one evening after work. They needed just one more day of sunshine to reach their peak of on-the-vine sweetness.

I told my daughter to go pick the first ones. She raced over to the strawberry patch. A minute later she hollered, "Mama, I think the chickens ate them."

I walked toward the box. "There should be a whole bunch of ripe ones at the back of the box," I said. I figured they may have picked a few of the low-hanging berries outside of the raised box.

When I reached the box, my mouth dropped open. They'd literally eaten every single red or pink strawberry in the entire patch. Scratch marks littered the soil, evidence they'd managed to fly up into the almost two-and-a-half-foot tall raised boxes.

My cheeks burned. How dare those chickens eat our berries? I'd waited weeks for them to get ripe. I marched out into the field and let them know they'd all be going into the stew pot if they touched my berry patch again. And they'd be sequestered to the chicken tractor pen for the season as well.

My daughter followed me. "Mama, are you mad at those chickens?"

"Yes, I am. They ate all our berries."

She looked at them. "Are you really going to butcher them?"

I shook my head. "Not right now."

The next morning I didn't let them out of their ranging pen before work. I didn't trust them not to raid my patch again. Truthfully, I was still a bit miffed at them.

As I drove to work, I calmed down a bit. I also realized they may have eaten all my strawberries, which have about a four-week window here, but they give me eggs every day of the year. Perspective.

When I got home from work, my husband had taken netting and tacked it over the strawberries. The hens were allowed to free range again, and I could still have my strawberries.

$$* * *$$

I grew up on a cattle farm. At the height of my father's herd, he ran about 130 cattle. To some of you that may seem like a lot, to others, just small potatoes. To me, it was simply the way I grew up.

During the winter months I went with my father every night when he got home from hauling logs up the road to our barn. To this day I can close my eyes and remember the sweet, musty scent of hay, damp winter air hugging my cheeks, and the spongy feel of decades of loose hay squishing beneath my booted feet. In the beginning of winter, the stacks of hay stretched clear up into the rafters of the old barn.

I scaled those stacks as nimbly as Spiderman ever dreamed. Our barn was built sometime in the late 1800s and no electricity was ever put in. When the sun dropped behind the mountain ridge in late afternoon, hours before the workday was done, my father would shine a flashlight up into the stacks to guide my hands and feet.

Straw poked my fingers. Tight baling twine left momentary red marks. I'd push the bales down and they'd topple end over end before dropping with a muffled thud to the ground below. If I missed and hit the side of the truck bed, the bale would usually split open. If it was a heavier bale, it'd leave a small dent in the metal. Good thing farm trucks aren't expected to look pretty.

After all the bales were on the ground, my dad would load the back of the truck. In the middle of winter, we'd usually feed the cows about thirty bales. Once the bales were loaded I'd push and tug them into place. I learned pretty quickly my legs were stronger than my arms. If a bale was too heavy, I'd hold onto the bed of the truck and shove with booted feet against the bale until it was in place.

I learned to drive a stick shift when I was about nine years old. My father said if I learned on a stick I'd never have a problem driving an automatic. He was right. I also learned not to pop the clutch. If you've ever thrown your dad off the back of the truck you'll quickly develop the finesse of slowly letting the clutch out while feathering the gas.

When I was younger, I'd drive the truck while my father tossed the hay off the back. He also used this time to check on the herd. We dropped flakes of hay like a trail of breadcrumbs behind us. The head of the herd filed in first, bellowing and jostling for position for the first bites.

Younger cows kicked up their heels and bounced along the edge of the herd until more hay was tossed for them. You'd think they'd remember from the night before that everyone got fed, but they were never patient.

It took over a half hour to get all the feed on the ground. Every night I'd drive over a different section of the field. This kept us from putting the feeding where they'd gone to the bathroom the previous night and also worked to make sure all of the pasture received fertilization in the form of their manure and the leftover bits of hay that would turn into compost come spring.

When we were done, my father would holler. I'd bring the truck to a stop and slide over. He'd climb into the truck, smelling of hay and freshly cut wood, the perfume of a farmer and logger rolled into one. Rough hands warmed against the heater vents. He'd roll down the driver's side window and drive back along the line of cattle, headlights shining like lanterns, reflecting in the cattle's eyes. His gaze traveled over them, counting and noting which cows looked close to calving. If some were missing we went looking. It didn't matter that he'd been up since three that morning. We'd drive along the mountainside and down to the pond, searching for the lone cow.

Most times we'd find a mama cow holed up with her new calf. Occasionally we'd find a small or younger cow having trouble birthing. The closest veterinarian was over an hour away if they came the moment we called. In the time before cell phones, we'd have to leave the pasture and drive the mile or so back to our home.

Even if we'd had a cell phone, my father wouldn't have called. He's done all his own doctoring on his herd since he was a boy, same as his father before him. My father never hid the harder part of owning animals from me. Living on a farm, you learn the cycle of life and death.

There are occasions when you get there just in time. For a few years, we had a bull that threw calves with exceptionally large heads. This was fine for our older cows who'd birthed before. It wasn't so good on our younger first-timers.

One of our cows went into labor and had been for some time. It was apparent she wasn't going to last much longer. If she died, so would the unborn calf still inside her. The only way for both the calf and the mother to have a chance was to pull the calf.

Our cows weren't pets. We didn't go out and pet them, but in times of distress, they sensed we were there to help. "Easy there. We've got to get your baby out." My father patted the cow's flank as he spoke. Gauging her contractions, he waited to reach up and tie a rope around the calf's front hooves.

On the cow's next contraction, my father dug both boot heels into the muddy pasture and pulled. Into the world slipped a red-bodied, white-faced calf. My father wiped clear its nose. "Come on, little one. Breathe."

My own breath swelled in my chest. Would this one make it?

When its belly rose and fell I clapped my hands. It is a wondrous thing to witness life.

Occasionally, we wouldn't make it in time. That taught me to appreciate life all the more. Sometimes the mother would perish, leaving behind a newborn calf. While I was saddened by this, it meant we got to bring the calf home and bottle-feed it.

One of most memorable bottle-fed babies was a little steer we named Jumping Jack. My dad made a pen for him in the yard behind our trailer. When Jumping Jack saw us coming with his bottle, he'd get so excited he'd start jumping up and down like a four-legged pogo stick.

While he drank from the bottle, I'd run my fingers through his soft coat. When he was finished he'd butt against the bottle, seeking more. Even after he was old enough to be turned loose into the herd, Jumping Jack would still greet us at feeding time.

Spring and summer brought green pasture and the end of nightly feedings. On the back of extra daylight come mosquitos and fence fixing. It's easiest to build or fix fences in the early spring, before vegetation (specifically stinging nettles) has had a chance to sprint toward the sky. I helped carry fence posts up hills and down banks.

Despite the heat of August, a cattleman's mind is turned to the long stretch of winter and no fresh pasture. We hauled in loads of hay. Bits of straw and dust covered our sweaty arms and faces like dull glitter. Itchy glitter.

Even though it was work, a witness to both life and death, these are some of my richest childhood memories. I learned working side-by-side with my father who he was. I learned his beliefs. I learned things about my heavenly Father as well. Knowing how much work goes into tending a herd of cattle, this verse rings in my head.

> For every animal of the forest is mine, and the cattle on a thousand hills. I know every bird in the mountains, and the creatures in the fields are mine. If I were hungry I would not tell you, for the world is mine, and all that is in it (Psalm 50:10-12).

I've helped care for the cows on one hill. A very small hill. My husband and I own a small herd of six cattle. Even though we raise some of our animals for meat, it doesn't mean we are callous toward them. We care about their comfort. We are thankful for their sustenance. And because I know what level of care it takes to watch over and provide for mere animals, I understand a smidgen of what God does for us.

Coyotes are a natural predator where we live. We have signs of bears in the late summer, but rarely do we see them. There's only been one winter that I can recall where we had a cougar kill a cow in the neighboring pasture and attack a young horse a few miles up the road. So I don't generally worry about wild animals attacking my kids while they're playing in our backyard and the stretch of woods between the road and our home.

I roamed those woods myself as a kid. Vine maples were horses, a burnt-out old-growth stump became a house, and pinecones made a fine addition to my make-believe pantry. Devil's club and stinging nettles were a bigger threat than wild animals. Bits of moss and pine needles were my perfume.

This past summer proved to be a bit different. The coyotes increased in number. In the middle of the day they could be seen crossing the road. Shaggy coats and leggy strides carried them into the underbrush. Their yips echoed across the pasture and forest, like a high-pitched serenade, each proclaiming their spot. Usually sung in darkness, their notes invaded the daylight hours. It seemed they surrounded our property.

Two younger chickens both went missing the same night.

With the sun high overhead, the kids and I hunkered down in the small spot of shade behind the rows of green beans. Buckets turned upside-down for seats and bare toes buried down into the cool soil. *Plunk. Plink.* Beans thudded against our colanders and bowls.

"Did you see that?" My husband cut the engine to the lawn mower.

I glanced over my shoulder. "See what?"

"That coyote." He pointed toward the fence bordering our front yard. "It jogged from the woods and across the yard right past you. It was just a few yards from the garden. You didn't see it?"

My gaze followed his finger. A tiny chill tap danced up my spine despite the August heat. "No. We were picking the beans and didn't see it." While I don't fear coyotes, the idea of their being so close to my children in broad daylight sat with me as well as chopped onions on top of sugar cookies.

A brief breeze rustled the overgrown grass where the coyote had trotted. We went back to picking beans, but I tossed a glance over my shoulder every so often.

It wasn't much later that my husband and I were sipping coffee near our back porch. Summer mornings have a way of building. They stretch, like a baby just waking up, until the sun arches into its full position. The sun hung above the cottonwood trees in our back field.

The chickens meandered about the grass, their feathers a comforting sight against the browning pasture. I gasped.

As they clucked to one another, a large coyote crept up behind them. Oblivious to the danger behind them, they kept on grazing. I jumped to my feet. My pulse pounded.

My husband hurried to our gun safe. I lunged toward the sliding glass door. Could I reach the flock before one of them was snatched?

The coyote saw my movement. It loped toward the lower pasture where our mama cows and calves grazed. Our hens never saw the predator. They didn't have a clue they'd just been spared.

My husband walked the fence line. The coyote had left without claiming a victim.

My chickens have no idea all we do for them. They squawk at us when they want more food or don't think we've given them enough. When it suits them, they enjoy our presence. Other times we have a hard time getting them to come near. But this doesn't stop us from watching over them. When a sign of danger comes, we're quick to jump up and defend them.

As I watched our flock graze in the backyard, I realized how much God does for us we're not even aware of. He sees the coyote and moves to protect His people without our knowing. His gaze roams the pasture and He knows the instant the enemy encroaches on us.

One time the coyote came a-calling when I was hanging clothes on the line. "You get out of here," I yelled.

The coyote wasn't impressed with my yelling. In fact, he was so focused on his prey, he didn't even glance my way.

Adrenaline pumped through my limbs. I raced across the yard and through the fence. Empty-handed, I ran straight for that coyote. I don't have any idea what I planned on doing if the coyote didn't retreat, but I was not going to stand by and let him get one of my chickens. Either he was extremely hungry or not afraid to test my mettle.

Not until I was a mere 20 feet away did he turn and run back into the woods. I herded the chickens into the run-out pen. I sucked in a deep breath. My hands shook.

God will chase down coyotes for you. At the cross, Jesus ran head-on at the danger confronting you and overcame it. He is our Shepherd. I am glad I am one of His flock.

Getting Started

Two things to ponder when considering raising livestock:

First, which animals to raise. There are many options from laying hens, meat chickens, beef cattle, pigs, sheep, goats, rabbits, or even fish in ponds or large tanks. Laying hens are great because if you purchase hens instead of chicks, you're getting food every day from the get-go. The other livestock offer larger amounts of food, but some of them will be dependent on where you live and the amount of acreage you own. Goats can provide milk and meat. Rabbits are a good meat source and they breed quickly. If you've never had rabbit it tastes just like chicken. Sheep can be used for both their wool and meat. Fish provide meat as well.

Second, consider the end game. This will help you decide which livestock animals to start with. Do you want dairy animals? Then a goat or cow will be your choice. Do you want enough meat to feed your family for an entire year with one animal? Then beef cattle or pigs will most likely be your choice.

Don't want to spend an entire year or two caring for an animal? Then consider meat chickens that are ready to butcher and eat in as little as eight weeks. We raise Cornish Cross chickens as our meat bird. Many folks also like Freedom Rangers, though they take longer to reach butchering weight.

Fencing options

Cattle do well with both electric and barbed wire fencing. We use barbed wire as we have close to fifteen acres to fence, and a lot of that is filled with underbrush, which will short out electric fencing. There is also the cost of running an electric fence, but there are solar units available to help with the cost of electricity.

Barbed wire is best used on permanent areas of fencing, though it can be taken out if needed. You'll need fence posts, of course. The two most common are either metal T-posts that you pound into the ground and wooden fence posts. Wooden fence posts require digging a hole. If you're doing a few, a manual post hole digger works fine, but for long stretches of fence you'll want to look into renting a tractor with a hole digger on the back. When choosing wood, make sure you choose a variety that won't rot quickly, such as cedar or railroad ties. There are split rail fences made entirely of wood, but most people don't have access to that much wood or enough money to put in miles of this kind of fencing.

One note on barbed wire: If a cow can get their head through the wire, the rest of the body can and often will follow. We use four strands of wire for our fence. Make sure a strand is low enough to the ground the cow can't crawl under it. They do a mean belly crawl.

A good option to put in the middle of fence sections between posts are metal fence stays. They're a piece of twisted metal that keeps the wire from stretching when it's pushed or pulled. The top strand is best at about four feet, making it harder for a cow to jump over. (Though we've had some cows that must have been bred to a gazelle, because they jumped and cleared over four feet with room to spare.)

Electric fencing works well for pigs and horses. Cattle will also respect an electric fence. You need to make sure the fence is properly grounded and that no grass or other items are touching it, as this can cause the fence to short out.

No matter which type of fencing you choose, you'll still need to monitor it regularly and check for weakened areas, loose posts, or holes in the fence.

The main reason cattle get out of the fence or go through it is to get to fresh feed. If they don't have enough to eat and there is ample food just on the other side of the fence, they will go for the greener grass. If you have a bull nearby and a cow goes into heat, nature will take over and he will come calling, fence or no fence.

Clean and ample water is more important than food. Be sure to check water levels daily in hot weather. An automatic stock tank valve will keep your water tank at a certain level—you just connect your hose to the device. And a stock tank heater keeps water from freezing during frigid winter temperatures. An old bathtub makes an excellent water tank, and many times can be found for free when people are remodeling or renovating.

Breeding

With any livestock, you'll need to decide if you want to get into breeding yourself or purchase animals to replace those you butcher for food. We prefer to buy our animals from someone we know when possible in order to see the conditions of the farm and ask questions.

We breed our cows every year. There are three options for breeding: artificial insemination, having your own bull, or taking your cow to a bull. If you only have a few cattle, having a bull will likely be more of a cost than it's worth. That is the case for us. Because my father has a herd of about 30 cows, he still keeps a bull. We take our cows down to his bull when we're ready to have them bred.

We don't breed our own chickens or pigs. I purchase our pigs from a local breeder and have gotten all of our laying hens from friends who were thinning their flocks. We purchase our meat chickens from a family-run and operated hatchery.

While breeding is more self-sufficient, be sure you're ready to take on all that caring for a pregnant mother and babies entails, as well as managing the male breeding animal. Oftentimes the male is more aggressive, as with bulls, roosters, and bucks (male goats). It is their job to protect their flock or herd, and occasionally, there is one who is really aggressive.

When I was a little girl we had a bull who would charge people when they were in the field. We hadn't had him very long and none of our other bulls behaved like this. I was used to walking along the fence line in the pasture to go visit my grandma, who lived up the field from us. I had worn a trail in the grass and under the fence where I'd slide through into her yard.

One day I was walking in the field with my mom and a few of the neighborhood kids. I was the last one and dawdling in the field. My mom and the others had made it back through the fence into the yard.

All of a sudden my mother and the kids started yelling. "Run! Get out of the way!"

I stood there, not having a clue what they were all hollering about. Slowly, I looked over my shoulder.

The bull was barreling toward me. His hooves pounded the dirt.

Fear rushed through my veins. The screams of my mom finally registered. I sprinted for the fence.

The bull was removed from our homestead promptly.

We've had other bulls who were like pets. My father could walk up and pet them and they followed him through the long grass like a dog. When owning livestock, you'll definitely want to observe the behavior of the animals before bringing them home and make sure your fences or pens are strong enough to hold them.

Beef

Most folks aren't able to raise their own beef. After all, it does require some property. Where we live, it takes about an acre of pasture per animal to avoid feeding hay all year long. (This will vary depending upon your climate.)

If you don't have property, leasing pasture from someone else is an option. Some farmers will allow you to purchase a cow from them and have you pay a certain amount to raise it for you. Another option is to just purchase the beef at butchering time for a set-upon amount per pound. This is the most common method where we are.

You can find small farmers who sell a whole, half, or quarter of a beef each fall. Ask friends who they purchase from or if they know of anyone who has extra to sell. Social media makes this extremely easy as multiple people can answer and point you in the right direction at once.

Pigs

Pigs are a good alternative to cattle if you have less land but still want a large amount of meat while only raising a few animals. We've found it's the same amount of work to raise two pigs and it keeps them from being lonely.

If you get your piglets when the nights are still cold, you'll need to keep them under a heat lamp for the first couple of weeks. We've raised pigs in the winter and spring and it's definitely less work when they're raised through the warmer months.

Piglets will need some sort of shelter from the weather. We used an old crate and turned it on its side with a tarp over the top and sides to create a dry and shady area. Pigs don't sweat, so it's also important for them to have a way to keep cool during the hotter months. This is why pigs like to wallow in mud holes; it helps cool them off. Our pigs love to play in the water and will jump into the water trough until just their snouts are sticking out. If you spray water out of the hose, they'll run through like a couple of kids in a sprinkler.

Pigs also like to root, so they'll quickly plow any area they're penned up in. If you have an area of ground you want worked up for a new garden plot or to get rid of brush, consider putting part of your pig pen there. Because they don't just eat the vegetation, but actually dig it up with their snouts, they're better at clearing brush than goats. You'll also receive free fertilizer in the form of their manure.

When they're small, you'll want to use wire mesh fencing. Once they're older (big enough they won't walk right under the bottom strand), you can use barbed wire fencing. However, they can root down and under the fence, so you'll want to run a strand of hot wire along the bottom of the fence near the ground.

Pigs love fruit and vegetables. We plant extra summer and winter squash to feed our pigs and roast a couple of large zucchini in the summer to feed them daily. Instead of a grain- or corn-based diet, we feed our pigs vegetables, barley, and even hay. When the apples come on, we pick up all the fallen ones from neighbors' and families' trees. We think it gives the meat a sweeter flavor.

Pigs will eat any table scraps, but we don't feed them anything with meat in it. While our pigs don't have as much fat on them as corn-fed pigs, the taste in the meat is well worth it. They like bread as well, but just as with people, a diet rich in vegetables and fruit is best.

Check with your local grocery stores for produce beyond its prime.

Many will allow you to come and pick up unsalable items. If you have any farms nearby you might also check with them for unsalable produce. Now, you don't want to be feeding your pigs rotten food. The meat will taste like what they've been fed. But slightly past prime is fine.

Chickens

I've heard it said chickens are a gateway animal to wanting a full-on farm. Like many things in life, I went at this backward. We started out with cattle, raised pigs, and then added chickens.

If you'd like to try your hand at chickens and you live within city limits, you'll need to check out city ordinances. Many cities will allow you to have a few chickens, but you'll want to double-check for your area. You may also want to check with your neighbors if you live in close quarters. Most folks don't mind listening to chickens squawk (and they do) if they get a dozen free eggs from time to time. Think twice about a rooster. Squawking is one thing; a rooster crowing in the wee hours of the morning is quite another.

If you live out on a farm like us, you can get as many chickens as your heart desires…or as your patience allows. I recommend starting out with already-laying hens. You may pay a little bit more, but it's far worth it in my opinion. Having raised two flocks, we've had much more success with purchasing older hens.

The chicks are cute. All the soft, downy fluffballs are sweet as they toddle about, but they're a lot more work. You must provide them with a heat lamp until their feathers come in. They don't begin to lay eggs until about four to five months old, so you'll be paying for feed and care without any eggs in return. Because they're young, they're more likely to get into trouble. Older hens are more cautious and watch out for predators.

Starting with already laying hens also ensures you won't accidently end up with hens that have suddenly turned into roosters. I know many an unsuspecting person who has thought she was buying hens and ended up with four roosters by mistake. But if you plan on letting your hens hatch out baby chicks, then a rooster isn't such a bad idea. Roosters also tend to protect the flock.

However, roosters like to crow. I like to sleep in when I can. See the conflict?

Too many roosters will also lead to worn-out hens, and some people are bothered by fertilized chicken eggs. They will have blood spots in them if they're starting to develop baby chicks.

We choose not to have a rooster at this time.

Meat Chickens

Heritage breed chickens take longer to raise, resulting in a higher cost of feed and an older bird by the time they're ready to butcher. This isn't all bad, as they're easier to come by and can be used for both eggs and meat.

White Cornish broilers are a hybrid chicken, meaning they've been raised specifically for meat and selectively bred (not genetically modified) for traits of growing quickly and having a lot of meat. They are ready to be butchered at just eight to ten weeks of age.

We decided to go with the White Cornish broilers due to their short raising period. You can either mail order chicks or purchase them from a store in the spring. We've purchased our meat chicks from both a local feed store and family-owned hatchery.

Baby chicks can be shipped through the mail at birth because when chicks hatch, they don't need food or water for the first three days of life. (In the wild, not all of the eggs hatch at the same time. A hen can't leave her unhatched eggs to tend to the hatched chicks, or the rest of the chicks will die before hatching.) So hatcheries can ship out chicks on the day they're hatched even if they won't reach their destination for a couple of days.

You should call your post office to let them know your chicks are on their way so they can call you the moment the chicks arrive in the morning.

10 Tips for Raising Meat Chickens

1. Inspect before you buy. If purchasing from a store, be sure you see the chicks up and walking before loading them. One of the chicks in our most recent dozen had a broken leg. It was lying down when we purchased it and we didn't see the injury until we got home. It died within a day.

2. Have a heat lamp ready. When chicks only have their down, they need a heat lamp to keep warm. It's also important to have them in a pen or area without corners. Chicks can become trapped in corners and trampled by the other birds. They'll need the heat lamp until their feathers come in, usually about three weeks with meat birds.

3. Be prepared to feed a lot. If you're used to raising regular laying hens, be prepared to feed much more often and use a lot more feed. Our hens will go through their feed in about four days. The meat chickens went through the same amount in a day. Take away their feed at night to help establish healthy eating habits and avoid organ failure.

4. Keep the water full. Just like their feed, they go through a lot more water. Be sure they have plenty of fresh water in their pen.

5. Be sure they have shade. Their feathers are slower to come in and they have light skin. If you let them out into a run or pasture, keep food and water in the coop and where they're ranging.

6. Don't back out. Once you have the meat chickens, do

not change your mind about butchering them. They're bred to be raised to a maximum of ten weeks. If you go over this, their legs will break and give out due to the weight of their bodies. Or they'll have heart failure. The whole point of raising your own meat is to be humane. Don't let them suffer because you got cold feet.

7. Mark the calendar. Count out from when you purchased the chickens to their full maturity date of eight to ten weeks. Many county extension offices have chicken butchering equipment for rent at reasonable rates, but you have to reserve it in advance.

8. Only dish up healthy feed. Be sure and purchase only unmedicated feed for your chickens. We purchased organic feed to be sure they weren't getting GMO products in their food. Remember, you're going to be eating what they're eating.

9. Keep their pens clean. Don't stuff your birds into a tiny living area. Be sure they have room to move about. It's best for them to run around on pasture. If that's not possible, be sure there's enough space for them to spread out and for you to keep it clean. Also be sure there is adequate ventilation.

10. Don't become attached. Anytime we're raising animals for food, we don't think of them as pets. We don't name them. We do make sure they're cared for and treated humanely. Our children know upfront the animals are for food. We don't lie, fib, or try to hide the fact. Our children are very well adjusted with the fact we raise our own food, and they know what that entails.

You'll need to provide some sort of coop for your chickens. They'll need nesting boxes and a place to roost. Plenty of clean water and feed is also necessary. Chickens love vegetable and fruit scraps, and they'll clean up your yard of bugs as well. But they might beat you to the ripe strawberries and tomatoes. They also like bread. Truthfully, they'll eat just about anything. You can help keep your feed bill down by supplementing with kitchen scraps and garden extras.

Chickens scratch, a lot, mainly the ground, but occasionally each other. They'll scratch a hole in your flowerbeds like a dog burying a bone. If you like manicured lawns and flowers, you won't want free-ranging chickens.

But for the work they require, there is nothing like farm-fresh eggs. Even the organic pasture-raised eggs you buy from the store don't compare to the eggs straight from your own backyard. The yolks are a deep orange and I swear they taste better.

When my chickens went through their molting period this past fall and didn't lay eggs for a month, I had to purchase eggs from the store. It had been years since I bought eggs, and when I cracked one open and saw a pale yellow yolk, I stared at it in confusion for a moment. *This isn't how eggs are supposed to look*, I thought.

I whispered a prayer of thanks when my girls started laying faithfully again. My baked goods returned to their normal richer color and flavor.

When left to free range, our chickens especially like to be wherever we are. They talk. A lot. I've been known to carry on a good conversation or two myself, but our chickens can out-talk even me. I'm not quite so fond of their constant chattering.

Especially when I'm trying to relax and find quiet.

I seek solitude outdoors. When I'm outside I see the rain clouds forming on the horizon, the misty cloud works its way down the ridge in a visible wall toward our home. Sunlight filters through and rainbows, sometimes two together, stretch across the valley. Leaves unfurl in the spring; in fall they dance around our feet. In the deep of winter frost patterns more intricate than any painting whirl over a silent land. But it can be a little bit hard to stand in that awe when you have a flock of noisy chickens cackling at your feet and dodging your every step. Some of this may be my fault as they're usually searching my hands to see if I hold any treats of apple scraps or bread ends.

Too often I'm looking for the perfect moment to see God. But He speaks to us no matter how many cows are bawling and chickens flapping in the dust. Sometimes, He speaks to us through the chickens running away from us as we chase them with a bedsheet.

About that bedsheet, here's the story.

Throughout the spring and summer we let our chickens range free on our property. This simply means they're not kept in any kind of cage. The door to the coop and run-out pen is left open and they can enter and leave at will. We purchase very little feed from the store as chickens love to forage for insects and plants. You know those big old nasty black carpenter ants that crawl out from seemingly every rock and log on the first hot day of spring? We had no ants invading our deck this year. If you've ever had these ants besiege your home, make it into your bed, and pinch the dickens out of you while trying to fall asleep, you'll know the joy I felt upon seeing the chickens gobble them up.

Fall came with crispy mornings, the crunch of frozen grass underfoot, and my chickens no longer laying their eggs in the coop. They would roost at night but laid their eggs in other areas of the yard. We found one spot behind a clump of grass on top of rocks. None of the eggs were broken, cradled by sharp stones instead of soft straw. Another hen decided to lay her eggs next to a tractor wheel.

Much as I hate to admit it, they managed to hide their eggs so well we couldn't find them. Since we don't have a rooster to fertilize the eggs it didn't matter where the hens hid them—no baby chicks would be hatching.

Watching the weather forecast, we had a week-long stretch of temperatures dropping into the single digits at night without climbing much higher during the day. We plugged in the heat lamp for the chickens and the water trough heater. The coyotes were also moving in, and I wanted my girls safe and snug.

All of my chickens but one happily went into the coop and run-out pen. Clucky, a Buff Orpington breed (the kids named her), managed to fly up into our grape arbor every evening at dusk, just out of reach, refusing to be caught. Normally friendly, she seemed to know I wanted to catch her and would let me get within about two feet before running off.

After two days of trying to coax her with treats and sweet talk, I decided enough was enough. When she came down off her roost in the morning I'd get her. I'd just turned on the water to jump in the shower when she made her descent. Perhaps chickens have better hearing than we think.

I tied my bathrobe tightly over my pajamas and slid into my rubber boots. Bedsheet in hand, I tromped out the door. "Come here, Clucky. That's a good girl." My voice sounded as sweet as golden honey on a buttermilk biscuit.

My fingers gripped the flannel sheet. I'd toss it over her like a large net rather than try and scoop her up outright. I inched closer. Clucky darted left.

I tossed my sheet.

Like a parachute, it ballooned out and slowly floated to the ground. Even an arthritic chicken with a walker could have eluded it. Flannel sheets don't have much weight to them, apparently.

My blood pumped. My plan might not have been the best, but I was committed now. I yanked the sheet up and tiptoed up to Clucky, who was peeking out from behind a bush in the flowerbed against the house. This was good. She was trapped against the house and couldn't get away from the sheet as fast.

Have you ever tried to creep in rubber boots? They're not exactly stealth-mode footwear, let me tell you.

Clucky squawked and wings a flapping, darted toward the end of the house. Certain I'd catch her at the end of the row, I waited in place.

I threw my sheet.

Clucky cleared the sheet and me, booking it to the front yard. She's a courageous chicken...or else I'm just not as formidable as I'd like to think.

I followed. Red-faced, I forgot any semblance of sneaking. "Get over here, Clucky. I mean it, right now."

We danced back and forth, like a calf and roper minus the grace. Her feather and wings twitched every which way and my bathrobe flailed. My gaze narrowed. I was going to catch this chicken if it took me all cotton-pickin' day.

I chased her through the front yard, into the driveway, back by the camper, in front of the hay bales, and finally, back to the backyard. We eyed each other.

I blocked her feint to the left. She flapped toward the blackberry vines.

I'd like to think my aim got better, but I think she was too tired to move as quickly. The sheet floated over her.

I scooped her up, still inside the sheet, and carried her through the gate and across the pasture. Both of us were out of breath. She curled into my side. I held her for a few minutes at the coop, her body warming my stiff hands through the fabric, her heartbeat slowing to a steady rhythm.

Opening the door to the nesting boxes, I set her inside. She glanced at me. With a few blinks she turned around and continued into the coop as if it had been her idea all along.

I shut the latch. "I'm expecting some eggs after all that fussing, Clucky."

Walking back to the house I realized I'd just spent close to a half hour chasing a chicken around the yard in my bathrobe. Good thing we don't live next to a busy highway. I'm pretty sure my neighbors are used to my antics.

Chapter 8

Traditions

There is a time for everything, and a season
for every activity under the heavens.

ECCLESIASTES 3:1

*Traditions are what connect us to our past and our future. They're a
way of remembering and honoring those who went before us. Traditions aren't just things we do on certain holidays, but actions
engrained in our daily lives.*

*In this chapter we'll share spiritual traditions, family traditions, and
ways to begin new traditions in your home.*

Does anyone else feel a certain kinship with Charlie Brown when he brings home the little spindly Christmas tree?

When I was growing up we never spent money on a Christmas tree. Living in the forests of the Pacific Northwest, it seemed ludicrous to purchase what grew all around us on our own property. But let me tell you, all evergreens are not created equal. The trees on our property were not groomed or trimmed. They grew with the stress of the weather and the environment around them.

Whatever seeds fell from the surrounding trees were what grew. Hemlock boughs drape like green lace, but they're not good for much else and are usually culled for more profitable and desirable wood. White fir and blue spruce make the prettiest Christmas trees, but cedar and pine grow the most abundantly around our home. Most trees stretched much too tall to fit under the short roof of our trailer.

We'd finally find one spindly tree that met the height requirements and drag it back to the house. My mother liked the tree to sit in a corner so she could hide the most pitiful side of the tree against the wall. (I've known some people who will drill a hole in the tree and stuff a branch into it to fill the bare spots. We never went this far.)

As a child, I never saw the tree with a critical eye. One of my favorite Christmas traditions is decorating the tree. I love the twinkle of lights and sparkle of red and white against dark green branches. The house smells like the forest, crisp and sharp. An anticipation of the season wrapped into a scent.

Our tree might not have been the grandest, but to me, those spindly branches were lush and beautiful. Just like Charlie Brown, I gazed upon our tree with love. When we look at something with love, it becomes transformed—redeemed into something whole, beautiful, and treasured.

My husband's family tradition was to hike miles through tree farms or drive up mountain roads to find the perfect tree. It was an all-day affair. Caps and hats were worn so you could mark a tree as a *maybe* with your hat and continue on. Alas, many a hat was lost on the hunt.

Snow-caked boots and pant legs. Fingers stiffened in the cold. Up logging roads and steep switchbacks, their truck would chug through the ruts and snow. My father-in-law drove a log truck for a living, and handling the roads with a pickup was easy.

After hours of tromping through the woods they'd finally find the perfect tree. My mother-in-law remembers standing with all the kids on the side of the mountain while my father-in-law turned the truck around in the narrow icy lane. She waited until it was pointing back the correct way before letting the kids tromp back inside.

The mountain roads and woods have given shape to my family's traditions.

Many times we think of traditions in concordance with holidays. Certain dishes are prepared for Thanksgiving, Christmas, and Easter. Some families open all the presents on Christmas Eve, some on Christmas day, others open one present only on Christmas Eve.

But these traditions are brought out only certain times of the year. What of the traditions you and I perform every day? I think our weekly or daily traditions say much more about us than our holiday traditions.

We try to eat our supper together as a family at the dinner table. This was how we ate most nights when I was a child. My husband's family also ate together. He remembers having to ask if he could be excused from the dinner table. Eating a meal together at the table is a form of tradition.

Many of us cleave to our family traditions. They're memories and acts that define us. They tie us to loved ones, strengthening bonds every time we partake in the tradition. A tradition is a shared memory, a way of reaching back through time and loss. It's establishing a connection with our children. A way to make sure that what we hold dear is carried on after we're gone.

Are prayers part of your tradition? Is taking everything before the Lord something you're handing down to the next generation in your family? My mother is a woman of prayer. Every night before bed she led me through prayers. It's a tradition I continue with my own children. Every night when my head nestles the pillow I still say my prayers. I can't go to sleep without first talking to God.

Maybe your childhood family left you with unhealthy traditions—patterns of behavior that hurt instead of lifting up. Unlike some of the traditions that have been passed down from our earthly family, godly traditions are only there for our benefit. And like our earthly traditions, we have a choice if we will keep them or not.

New Year's Day

We enjoy getting together with our neighbors on New Year's. Laughter and streaks of children run by. A smorgasbord of food is set out and grazing is highly encouraged for hours on end. Games are played and relationships enriched.

My kids always look forward to New Year's Eve and frequently ask when it is. It's not any certain thing we do or food we serve, but the time spent with people. This is a tradition I hope they'll carry on and remember, not just at New Year's, but every day of their life.

Valentine's Day

My husband and I exchange cards on Valentine's Day with handwritten notes, and there is usually chocolate involved. Okay, there is always chocolate involved.

We don't do a big thing or gifts on Valentine's Day because I truly believe the best gift we can give one another is to show our love every day. It's not big sweeping gestures, though those have their place, but the little things we do for each other throughout the days and weeks of the year. And one of those things should involve chocolate.

A different frosting can totally transform a cake into something new and exciting. I love to pour this simple chocolate ganache recipe overtop a round cake. It looks decadent and tastes even better than it looks. (Because a cake should always taste as pretty as it looks.)

Easy Chocolate Ganache

1 cup heavy cream
8 ounces semisweet or dark chocolate, chopped

Place chocolate chips or chunks in a heatproof bowl and set aside. Over medium heat, bring cream to just barely a boil. Pour hot cream over chocolate and whisk until smooth and incorporated. Allow ganache to cool a touch until it's still warm, but not hot, and then pour over your cake.

Note: Chill the cake before making the ganache, as it will adhere better to a cold cake.

Easter

Easter Sunday is always one of my favorites. It celebrates the greatest gift ever given to mankind. I love seeing the pews brimming with people.

I am not a morning person. But Easter morning I'm up early as we hide Easter eggs throughout the house along with the kid's Easter baskets. However, when one is hiding eggs at dawn, one may grab a carton of uncooked eggs. Because our hens lay brown speckled eggs, in the early dawn, one might not notice. This made for an especially intense hunt because we didn't notice until after all the eggs were hidden...in my living room. Thankfully, all were accounted for and none were cracked.

We always have a family dinner on Easter, and it is not considered dinner unless we have homemade rolls. And my secret to perfectly risen rolls is baking them in a large cast-iron skillet. I even bake my cinnamon rolls in cast-iron skillets.

Below is my favorite homemade roll recipe.

Dinner Rolls

½ cup warm water

2¼ teaspoons yeast

½ cup buttermilk

1 egg

½ cup butter, softened

¼ cup honey

1 teaspoon salt

2 cups whole wheat flour (2½ cups if using spelt)

1¾ cup all-purpose flour

Pour warm water over yeast in a large bowl. Let sit for 5 minutes or until foamy. Add milk, egg, butter, and honey. Stir in salt and flour. Knead for 6 to 8 minutes. If not using a stand mixer with the kneading attachment, place a little bit of olive oil on your kneading surface. Adding too much flour when using whole wheat results in a dense product.

After kneading, place dough in an oiled bowl, cover, and let rise for an hour.

Punch dough down and form into rolls. Place rolls in a large cast-iron skillet. When rolls are touching, it forces them to rise up instead of out. Place the rolls in your oven with the light on and allow to rise about 45 minutes, or until doubled.

Remove skillet from oven and preheat oven to 400 degrees. Bake for 12 to 15 minutes. As soon as rolls come out of the oven, brush them with a stick of butter.

Fourth of July

When I was growing up, my father threw the biggest Fourth of July barbecue in the valley. A gaggle of campers gathered on our property along the river and folks would drive in until the field looked like a used car lot.

My father and the older boys would head down to the sandbar as soon as the sun set with boxes of fireworks. For close to an hour fireworks filled the darkened sky. Rain or shine, we ran through the pastures, grass seed sticking to socks and sand filling shoes. Wood smoke perfumed the air with makeshift tables laden with food.

For me, it's not the Fourth of July without a campfire, friends, and fireworks. And usually a stray firework or two that has you ducking when it goes off in the wrong direction or the rocket falls over.

A lot of people will talk about something being "as American as apple pie," and as much as I love apples and pie, the Fourth of July for me is all about raspberries. There's nothing like a recipe that allows fresh fruit to shine through.

Raspberry Cream Whip

1 pint heavy cream
¼ cup sugar (you could substitute honey or even maple syrup)
1 to 2 cups raspberries

In a stand mixer, whip cream until it thickens. Add in sugar to taste and continue to whip until stiff peaks form. Fold in raspberries. Spread over your favorite cake in place of frosting. It's delicious on chocolate cake and angel food cake...or by the spoonful.

Thanksgiving

The holiday retailers would have us forget in lieu of Christmas purchasing. But Thanksgiving is a day dedicated to the act of gratitude.

Give thanks in all circumstances; for this is God's will for you in Christ Jesus (1 Thessalonians 5:18).

Thanksgiving reminds us to focus on the things we do have and the gifts we have been given, not on the things we want or long for. It encapsulates how we should face every day and every situation in our lives.

Our Thanksgiving dinner is spent with my husband's family and in the evening, we go to my parents' home for dessert. I'm in charge of bringing apple pie. Actually, I'm kind of under direct orders from my father-in-law to bring apple pie. I double the recipe below and bring one to each side of the family.

I'm partial to Gravenstein apples, but you're not likely to find them in a grocery store. If my parents' tree didn't produce enough, I also like Gala, Honeycrisp, or Fuji apples for pies.

Old-Fashioned Apple Pie

2 pie crusts (recipe on page 121)
3 cups sliced apples (about 3 to 4 medium apples)
1 Tablespoon flour
⅓ cup sugar
½ teaspoon cinnamon
¼ teaspoon nutmeg
butter

Preheat oven to 400 degrees. Roll out pie crust and line a 9-inch pie plate or cast-iron skillet. Mix apples with flour, sugar, cinnamon, and nutmeg. Turn into pastry-lined pie plate. Top with four to six pats of butter.

Roll out top pie crust and place over apple filling. Crimp the edges of the pastry closed and cut slits to allow the steam to vent. Brush the top of the crust with a bit of milk or cream and sprinkle with a light dusting of sugar.

Bake for 50 minutes.

Christmas

I am like a child at Christmastime. I love the decorations, the twinkle of lights, the secret of gifts for those we hold dear, the nip in the air, and red and white peppermint sticks.

I usually put our tree up the first part of November so I can enjoy it for the entire season. It is an artificial tree—due to our woodstove, a live tree would dry out before Christmas and create a fire hazard. I can't abide not having the house smell like a Christmas tree, though, so I use essential oils in my diffuser and live boughs for wreaths. As our children age and are able to follow in my husband's family tradition of hunting down the perfect tree in the wilds, we'll adapt that route.

We do purchase store-bought gifts for our children and each other, alongside homemade ones. Most of the gifts I give to other family and friends are homemade. I cherish homemade gifts. The time and thoughtfulness that went into them warms my heart like a crackling fire on a windswept January night. In fact, those jars of jams, pickles, and some of the homemade sugar scrubs makes a fabulous homemade gift basket.

Last year I made homemade vanilla extract for my mother, my mother-in-law, and my husband's grandmother. Homemade extracts are extremely easy to make at home and aren't cut with water, sugar, or other additives.

Extracts are made with alcohol. The alcohol prevents most bacteria from growing and is the vehicle for the extracted flavor. The alcohol evaporates during baking.

Homemade Vanilla Extract

7 to 10 vanilla beans
**8 ounces vodka or rum (I like the flavor the rum gives
the vanilla)**

Run a knife lengthwise down the center of the bean to open it up. Chop the vanilla bean into 1-inch pieces. Place chopped vanilla beans into a clean pint-sized Mason jar. Pour alcohol over the beans until they're completely submerged. Put a lid on it and shake.

Place jar in a cool, dark spot (I use our cupboard near the sink where we store our coffee). Shake it every few days or so for about six weeks. You can go longer for a more intense flavor. Once extract has reached its desired strength, strain out the used beans and store in a clean glass jar. I purchased a couple of swing-top glass bottles to store my extract in and put one whole split bean inside to infuse a little extra flavor. Bake up as many wonderful things as you can imagine!

There's just something about Christmas and peppermint. They go together like freshly fallen snow and a moonlit night.

You can make this extract with fresh or dried leaves. I grow several kinds of mint and each variety will create a slightly different-tasting extract. When using fresh leaves, it's best to pick the leaves in the early morning as they contain the highest concentration of the oil.

Homemade Mint Extract

¾ to 1 cup of mint leaves
vodka

Rinse leaves and pat dry. Roll and crush each leaf between your fingers to release the oils. Alternatively, you can roughly chop them. Place leaves in a clean glass jelly jar.

Pour vodka over top until leaves are fully submerged. Place your lid on the jar and give it a good shake or two. Store the jar in a dark cupboard and shake it every few days.

Allow leaves to steep for at least six weeks, or longer for a stronger extract. Once extract is at desired strength, strain out the leaves and store in a clean glass jar out of sunlight and away from heat. For gift giving, I like to use a small chalkboard label to pretty up the jar.

Hosting

If you've ever thrown a get-together or party, as hostess, you want to make sure there's enough food to go around. Most of our barbecues and meals are potlucks. In fact, potlucks are one of my very favorite things. You get to try new dishes and there's usually a mountain of food without your having to cook it all. I've often thought life should be like a potluck, where everyone brings their best and shares.

However, sometimes not everyone brings something or extra guests come. I enjoy a large group. I'm a talker and when you grow up with a family of ten siblings, big gatherings feel natural. But when you're hosting, you begin to scan the food table. *What if there's not enough food? What do I have inside I can whip up quickly? We ran out of punch. I don't have enough forks.*

If you're not careful, you've worried yourself right out of a time of fellowship and enjoyment. I tend to be a Martha instead of a Mary at first reaction. It's a human reaction. The disciples reacted much the same way.

But we have a Jesus tradition to follow if we choose.

> Jesus called his disciples to him and said, "I have compassion on these people; they have already been with me three days and have nothing to eat. I do not want to send them away hungry, or they may collapse on the way."
>
> His disciples answered, "Where could we get enough bread in the remote place to feed such a crowd?"

I smile because I am so like the disciples. "Jesus, are you kidding? I've looked everywhere. There's no way I can fix this."

> "How many loaves do you have?" Jesus asked.
>
> "Seven," they replied, "and a few small fish."

To get some scope, there were four thousand men there. That's some gathering. Can you imagine if you were the event coordinator? Only seven loaves of bread for that many people. Major fail.

> Then he took the seven loaves and the fish, and when he had given thanks, he broke them and gave them to the disciples, and they in turn to the people. They all ate and were satisfied.

Jesus took what he had. He didn't stand there and whine about not having enough. He didn't throw up his hands and say, "Well, there's not enough so it's pointless to try."

He gave thanks.

He gave thanks before the food was multiplied. Before the crowd was satisfied. Before the miracle had taken place.

This is a tradition of both thanks and faith.

When you feel you don't have enough of something—patience,

money, food, whatever it is—thank God for the portion He's given you. And then with faith, ask Him that it would be enough to provide for the needs in front of you.

Don't do this expecting God to double or triple your bank account. Do this expecting He will meet your needs in *His* way. And have faith that it will be better than you could have planned.

Acknowledgments

The writing and birthing of a book is just as much a story as the book itself. There have been many individuals who helped write on the pages of my life and are a part of my story. My thanks to all these people and many more...

To my husband and children. I'm blessed beyond words by you. Thank you for your love and support.

To my mother, who read to me every night from the time I can remember. You instilled a love of books in me long before either of us knew what it would lead to.

To my father, who taught me the value of hard work. Your memories and knowledge of the old ways ensure they won't be forgotten and are passed on to others.

To my editor, Kathleen, whose vision brought this book into being and honed it into the work you hold in your hands. A more kindred spirit I couldn't find, and I'm grateful for her guidance.

To my agent, Sarah Joy Freese, for believing in me through many books and rewrites, and for meeting with patience my questions and moments of passing panic.

To Colleen L. Reece. If it weren't for your seeing the potential in my writing, I would have given up this dream forever. Thank you for following God's leading and your red editor's pen.

To Anne Schwartz. Thank you for sharing your gardening expertise and dedicating your work to being a good steward of the land and teaching others about organic practices.

To all of my readers who have sent notes of encouragement, stories, or just to say hello. I'm honored you let me be a part of your lives.

To my heavenly Father. Thank You for drawing me to You and for Your mercy and grace.

Recipe Index

Homemade Cleaners

Homemade Body Care Products

o you ever come to the end of a book and not want it to end? You wish there was just a little bit more. Me too! So I created this special e-course just for you. See, I've gotten to the end of too many books and wanted just a little bit more. Sometimes it's just to tell the author how much I enjoyed the book and other times, I needed some direction.

If you've read the whole book, there are probably so many things you want to try and do differently. I'm so happy to hear that. When I first embarked on this made-from-scratch way of life, it seemed overwhelming. I didn't know where to start. At times I just wanted some encouragement and advice from others who were walking this journey with me. It can feel lonely if you're the first or only one in your family or group of friends to make these changes.

So I created a special FREE five-day fast track Made-From-Scratch Life e-course as my way of saying thank you for purchasing this book and spending your precious time with me.

How does it work?

Simply sign up here:

melissaknorris.com/made-from-scratch-life-bonus-e-course/

And over five days you'll get five e-mails from me with tips and articles on how to implement these changes into your life and kitchen without being overwhelmed. We'll have some fun inspiration and a thing or two involving Mason jars…because I just can't help myself when it comes to Mason jars.

I can't wait to meet you and hear about your transformations!

Return to Simple

Inspiring Your Faith and Pioneer Roots

If you love old-fashioned living and think we need to get back to the simple way of life, then my Pioneering Today podcast is for you. We'll talk about how our great-grandparents lived and how to capture that in our modern lives.

The Pioneering Today Podcast is where food is homegrown, Mason jars line our pantries, meals are made from scratch, and the soul is nourished. The bi-monthly podcast is dedicated to helping you implement the best of the pioneer lifestyle into your modern one. I hope you'll be inspired to grow your own food, cook real, traditional meals, increase your home food storage, consider livestock, and draw closer in your relationship with Jesus.

Subscribe at MelissaKNorris.com.

Connect with Melissa online!

 facebook.com/MelissaKNorris

 @MelissaKNorris

 @MelissaKNorris

 pinterest.com/MelissaKNorris

Melissa K. Norris inspires people's faith and pioneer roots with her books, podcast, and blog. Melissa lives with her husband and two children in their own little house in the big woods in the foothills of the North Cascade Mountains. When she's not wrangling chickens and cattle, you can find her stuffing Mason jars with homegrown food and playing with flour and sugar in the kitchen. Visit her at MelissaKNorris.com.

To learn more about Harvest House books and
to read sample chapters, visit our website:

www.harvesthousepublishers.com

HARVEST HOUSE PUBLISHERS
EUGENE, OREGON